THE LYRIC NOW

Also by
James Longenbach

PROSE

How Poems Get Made
The Virtues of Poetry
The Art of the Poetic Line
The Resistance to Poetry
Modern Poetry after Modernism
Wallace Stevens
Stone Cottage

POETRY

Earthling
The Iron Key
Draft of a Letter
Fleet River
Threshold

THE LYRIC
NOW

James Longenbach

The University of Chicago Press   Chicago and London

The University of Chicago Press, Chicago 60637
The University of Chicago Press, Ltd., London
© 2020 by The University of Chicago
All rights reserved. No part of this book may be used or
reproduced in any manner whatsoever without written
permission, except in the case of brief quotations in critical
articles and reviews. For more information, contact the
University of Chicago Press, 1427 East 60th Street,
Chicago, IL 60637.
Published 2020
Printed in the United States of America

29 28 27 26 25 24 23 22 21 20   1 2 3 4 5

ISBN-13: 978-0-226-71599-5 (cloth)
ISBN-13: 978-0-226-71604-6 (paper)
ISBN-13: 978-0-226-71618-3 (e-book)
DOI: https://doi.org/10.7208/chicago/9780226716183.001.0001

Library of Congress Cataloging-in-Publication Data

Names: Longenbach, James, author.
Title: The lyric now / James Longenbach.
Description: Chicago : University of Chicago Press, 2020. |
Includes bibliographical references and index.
Identifiers: LCCN 2020007542 | ISBN 9780226715995 (cloth) |
ISBN 9780226716046 (paperback) | ISBN 9780226716183
(ebook)
Subjects: LCSH: American poetry—20th century—History
and criticism.
Classification: LCC PS323.5 .L66 2020 | DDC 811/.040905—
dc23
LC record available at https://lccn.loc.gov/2020007542

♾ This paper meets the requirements of ANSI/NISO
Z39.48-1992 (Permanence of Paper).

For Joanna

Contents

Preface

Who knows what a poem is? For the person beginning to write the poem as well as the person beginning to read it, the poem doesn't exist yet: the pleasure is an act of discovery, even if the writer has written a thousand poems preceding this one—even if the reader has read the poem at hand a hundred times. The title of this book may be read in two ways, but I mean the word *now* to function primarily as a noun, modified by an adjective—*the lyric now*: whether written in 1920 or 2020, a poem creates the moment as we enter it. The poem is happening now.

Like anyone who writes poems, I learned to do so by reading them; but more precisely, I learned to write poems by writing *about* them—often by writing about them again and again, since at different times the same poems have revealed themselves to me in different ways. Sometimes the appearance of new poems has forced me to reconsider a poet I thought I knew well; other times a new edition of old poems has seemed to reconfigure an entire career. The American poets I've written about here—Moore, Pound, Eliot, Stein, Williams, Oppen, Lowell, Bishop, Ashbery, Bidart, Graham, Phillips, Keith—have been acutely aware of one another's poems, and I have needed to inhabit that awareness myself. When one feels the need to read Marianne Moore or T. S. Eliot, do their poems feel any less present, less relevant, than those of Carl Phillips or Sally Keith?

Each of these poets has been in some way invested in the effort to "make it new," in Pound's famous phrase; for poets who came of age in the wake of modernism, novelty often became notoriety, though never for very long. Until it did not, Lowell's early embrace of meter and rhyme seemed radically new; and until it did not, Oppen's embrace of modernist strategies of fragmentation seemed old hat. In the 1950s or the 1990s, the fashionable young poet wrote rhymed quatrains; in the 1960s or the 2000s the same poet wrote disjunctive prose poems. And yet, like every decade preceding them, these decades produced poems whose authenticity does not depend on a resistance to another poem's power—poems that do not postulate an immortality contingent on another poet's obsolescence, as if mortality were for other people. A poem is the future, even if it exists in the past.

Over the past several decades, academic literary critics have debated the nature of the lyric poem with a fervor unseen since the heyday of the New Criticism, when the lyric lay at the center of our critical enterprise. This fervor has invigorated me almost as much as the ongoing project of lyric poetry, but my attention remains focused less on what the lyric is generally than on how a lyric works particularly, sentence by sentence, line by line: whatever else it may be, a poem is a work of art made of words, and the way in which a particular poem's language creates the repeatable event of itself is my preoccupation.

If the lives of the poets have sometimes proved to me as telling as their poems, it is nonetheless the event of the particular poem to which these tales attest. Equally telling has been the language of American musicians: the writings of Virgil Thomson and Patti Smith, musicians uncommonly involved with words, have offered me unexpected ways to describe what's happening in the poem that's happening now. We're used to listening to songs we love repeatedly, and poems we love, even poems long loved by other people, may assert their claim on our attention with similar persistence, often against our will.

Does the poem that's happening now make anything happen? As I write, near the end of the second decade of the twenty-first century, many poets consider poems to be a form of political intervention; there are very good reasons for wanting poems to function in this way, and there are equally good reasons, though less heartening ones, for wanting to know if poems can bear the weight of their maker's desires. Is a work of art made of words that meets the moment a lesser work when the moment passes? Why, having read such a poem by Virgil or Oppen, do we keep reading it?

Virgil flourished in the first century BCE. The earliest American poet I've written about here, William Carlos Williams, flourished more than one hundred years ago. One hundred years is a long time, longer than the life of most any poet; but within the ongoing history of lyric poetry, it's almost nothing. Once, to readers intent on evaluation, Williams seemed like an affront to available notions of both poetic and social decorum, and so did Wordsworth. But already the enthusiasms and antagonisms that preoccupied poets over the last several decades, much less the last century, have fallen away. What's left is the poetry: I've experienced some of its makers as contemporaries, each of them engaged in the act of arranging the raw material of language into art.

THE LYRIC NOW

I

Poet of Argument

On February 19, 1988, John Ashbery gave a poetry reading at the Folger Shakespeare Library in Washington, DC. Coincidentally, the Folger had mounted *Marianne Moore: Vision into Verse,* an exhibition that included an array of clippings and photographs Marianne Moore references in her poems—most prominently in "An Octopus," the longest poem in her 1924 volume *Observations.* Speaking extemporaneously, Ashbery called "An Octopus" the most important poem of the twentieth century, and when the remark provoked a few titters, he looked surprised: in his own mind he was reiterating a conviction neither novel nor idiosyncratic. "Despite the obvious grandeur of her chief competitors," he'd written two decades earlier, in a 1967 review of Moore's *Complete Poems,* "I am tempted simply to call her our greatest modern poet."

By chief competitors Ashbery meant the usual American modernist culprits—Pound, Eliot, Stevens, Frost, Williams—all of whom maintain a permanent claim on our attentions; with the notion that Moore belongs among this company no twenty-first-century reader could plausibly disagree. Not only the free-wheeling Ashbery but also the fastidious Richard Wilbur revered Moore's poems and, depending on how one approaches them, the poems themselves seem both freewheeling and fastidious. "She gives us," said Ashbery, "the feeling that life is softly exploding around us, within easy reach."

Moore was born near St. Louis, Missouri, in 1887. Her parents separated before her birth, and subsequently her father, already institutionalized, severed his hand, taking literally the injunction of Matthew 5:30 ("if thy right hand offend thee, cut it off"). To her mother and to her brother Warner, who became a Presbyterian minister, Moore remained fiercely, sometimes pathologically, close. She attended Bryn Mawr College, became a suffragette, moved to a tiny Greenwich Village apartment in 1918, and edited the legendary magazine *The Dial* from 1925 until its demise in 1929 (an achievement that would insure our interest in Moore, even if she had written no poems), but she lived with her mother until her mother's death in 1947. It's hard to imagine Marianne Moore sharing a bed with her mother while also composing her fiercely syntax-driven poems—

the spiked hand
that has an affection for one
and proves it to the bone,
impatient to assure you
that impatience is the mark of independence
not of bondage

—in which domestic relations often seem pointedly nightmarish.

Moore began publishing these poems around 1915, and immediately they were noticed by the modernist poets who became her peers, poets who would in turn write admiring essays about her work. Yet Moore remained mysterious. "Does your stuff 'appear' in America," asked Pound, after first encountering her poems in England. "Dear Mr. Pound," wrote Moore, "I do not appear." In 1921, her friend H. D. helped to arrange for the printing of a small collection called *Poems*, but Moore was neither involved with the publication nor pleased with the results. She held out as long as she could, finally publishing her first book, *Obser-*

vations, with the Dial Press in 1924; a slightly revised second edition appeared the following year.

Moore was a passionate reviser. Prior to being collected in *Observations*, her poems appeared in magazines in sometimes drastically different versions, and she continued to revise her poems for decades to come. Reading a poem from the 1920s in her 1967 *Complete Poems*, often one is in fact reading a poem from 1935 or 1951; in addition, because Moore's various selected and collected volumes omit some of the poems of *Observations*, the design of this volume—which is not merely a collection of discrete poems but a poetic multiverse of Whitmanian proportions—was for a long time obscured. More recent editions, attentive to Moore's editorial practice, allow us to see this masterpiece of American modernism whole.

What are the distinguishing features of *Observations*? Many people think of Moore as the author of intricately descriptive accounts of animal life, but the impression is largely due to the order that T. S. Eliot (acting in his capacity as an editor at Faber and Faber) devised for Moore's 1935 selected poems, an order to which she adhered in every subsequent selection: most people's experience of Moore begins with a group of long, descriptive poems written in the early 1930s ("The Steeple-Jack," "The Jerboa," "The Plumet Basilisk," "The Frigate Pelican"), followed by "The Fish," an arresting but, finally, untypical poem from *Observations*.

A fresh reading of *Observations* suggests that, while Moore's descriptive powers are formidable, she is primarily a poet of argument, which is to say, a poet of syntax—long, charismatic sentences whose convolutions often seduce us into agreement long before we have time to consider the substance of the argument at stake.

Consider the final two sentences of "England," typed out as if they were prose: despite the poem's title, Moore is discussing here the underestimated cultural richness of the country of her birth; more broadly, she's arguing against the tendency to associate any particular qualities with the supposed essence of a particular nationality.

> The sublimated wisdom of China, Egyptian discernment, the cataclysmic torrent of emotion compressed in the verbs of the Hebrew language, the books of the man who is able to say, "I envy nobody but him and him only, who catches more fish than I do,"—the flower and fruit of all that noted superiority—should one not have stumbled upon it in America, must one imagine that it is not there? It has never been confined to one locality.

What matters most about these two sentences is that the first is very long and the second is very short. Delaying its main subject and verb (*must one*) extravagantly, the first sentence begins with a list of noun phrases (*the sublimated wisdom; Egyptian discernment; torrent of emotion; the books of the man*), the noun phrases sometimes trailing dependent clauses (*who is able to say*), other times, modifying adjectival phrases (*compressed in the verbs of the Hebrew language*). All this information is gathered together in a final noun phrase (*the flower and fruit of all that noted superiority*), which then becomes the referent for the pronoun *it* in a dependent clause (*should one not have stumbled upon it in America*) preceding the long-delayed arrival of the sentence's subject and verb: *must one imagine that it is not there*. Must one imagine America to be bereft of the richness we associate clumsily with other cultures, the sentence asks, simply because we have not been attentive enough to perceive its presence?

The poem's final sentence, beginning tersely with its main subject and verb (*it has*), does not answer this question but reframes it: rather than allowing us simply to conclude that America must, on the contrary, be a place of noted superiority indeed, the sentence informs us straightforwardly that the flower and fruit of noted superiority has never been confined to one place. No nation—neither England, China, Egypt, nor America—has a special claim. This argument is extractable from the poem, but the syntax of the poem makes us participate in the act of the argument's construction, and, as a result, the poem feels like an ongoing act of thinking rather than a rehearsal of thought. The final sentence is a permanent surprise.

What happens when this sentence is cast in lines? Moore was an accomplished maker of prose sentences; the nearly seven hundred pages of her *Complete Prose* can be as exciting to read as her poems. But as a maker of poems, Moore often arranged her sentences in intricately designed stanzas—not so much to control as to heighten the extravagance of her syntactical flights. In this, she resembles John Donne, another poet of irresistible argument, except that Donne, like most English-language poets, organizes his lines by their number of metrical feet ("For *God*-sake *hold* your *tongue*, and *let* me *love*"). In contrast, Moore often organizes her lines simply by their number of syllables, allowing the stresses to fall in a variety of patterns. For instance, each stanza of "England" consists of four lines, containing twenty, fifteen, twenty-two, and eighteen syllables respectively, the first line rhyming with the third. As she originally lineated the final stanza, breaking the word *superiority* across the line—

to say, "I envy nobody but him and him only, who catches more
fish than
I do,"—the flower and fruit of all that noted superiority—should one not have stumbled upon it in America, must
one imagine
that it is not there? It has never been confined to one locality.

—the second line also rhymes with the fourth.

Is this stanza contrived? Is a sonnet contrived? Like any kind of aesthetic pattern, a poem's lines may threaten to seem arbitrary—that's paradoxically part of their power. It's tempting to suggest that Moore's stanzas are made for the eye; but if her lines and stanzas were not by their nature in a productive relationship with her syntax, determining its sound, then all poets—Moore, Donne, Ezra Pound—would simply write prose. All poetic lines introduce some additional pattern to the already highly patterned syntax of a poem's sentences, and if Moore's syllabic lines seem more contrived than Donne's metrical lines or Pound's free-verse lines, that's simply because we're less accustomed to them; there's no poetic form more weirdly arbitrary than the sonnet.

Throughout the first sentence of "Picking and Choosing," the length of the lines is determined by syllable count—

Literature is a phase of life: if
    one is afraid of it, the situation is irremediable; if
one approaches it familiarly,
    what one says of it is worthless.

—but Moore is not simply chopping up her syntax in order to obey the pattern, creating a visual experience; like any poet from Chaucer to Ashbery, she is shaping her syntax to take strategic advantage of what happens to it when the lines end.

Literature is a phase of life;
if one is afraid of it,
the situation is irremediable;
if one approaches it familiarly,
what one says of it is worthless.

This lineation, which I've imposed on the poem, sounds different from Moore's because these lines don't interrupt the integrity of the sentence's various clauses. Moore throws immense weight on the word *if* by dangling it at the end of two lines, and, as a result, the poem asks us to hear the sentence's intonation in one particular way and not another: "*if* one is afraid"—"*if* one approaches it familiarly." Moore's lineation similarly determines our experience of the thrilling conclusion of "England": after seven stanzas of incessant syntactical action, in which the length of the clauses and phrases are usually at odds not only with the ends of the lines but also with the ends of the stanzas, the poem's final line delivers us not only to the shortest sentence in the poem but also to the only sentence in the poem that is delivered to us whole and complete on a line: "It has never been confined to one locality."

"I am in perfect terror of Marianne," admitted her friend William Carlos Williams. Why would that be? These are a few of the many challenging tasks catalogued in "The Labors of Hercules."

to teach the patron-saint-to-atheists, the Coliseum
meet-me-alone-by-moonlight maudlin troubadour
that kickups for catstrings are not life
nor yet appropriate to death—that we are sick of the earth,
sick of the pig-sty, wild geese and wild men:
to convince snake-charming controversialists
that it is one thing to change one's mind,
another to eradicate it—that one keeps on knowing
"that the Negro is not brutal,
that the Jew is not greedy,
that the Oriental is not immoral,
that the German is not a Hun."

The author of these lines has zero patience for what Moore elsewhere calls "the storm of / conventional opinion," whether sentimental (maudlin poets spouting romantic clichés) or political (controversialists reveling in racial and national prejudice). Moore's sensibility mellowed with age, but, like Emily Dickinson, the poet of *Observations* is one of the most ferocious in the language, a poet whose passionate convictions are nailed to the page. The Jew is no more essentially greedy, the German no more predictably a Hun, than (as "England" argues) the American is shallow.

The lines I've quoted from "The Labors of Hercules" are written not in syllabic verse but in free verse, which Moore began to write around 1920. Why, after mastering her syllabic forms, did Moore shift her procedures, going so far as to reorganize a few of her earlier poems into free-verse lines? Linda Leavell, the poet's most recent biographer, suggests that Moore gave up syllabics because readers grown accustomed to free verse found her line breaks distracting, but it's impossible to imagine Moore succumbing to such craven motivations, and, in any case, she would return to syllabics in the 1930s with gusto. The very design of *Observations* itself tells a more convincing story.

The book is organized chronologically, but not simply by default. *Observations* begins with its simplest poems, poems that educate us in Moore's procedures, moving on to longer poems cast in more elaborate syllabic stanzas. Within this group, the structures of the poems begin to change: increasingly the poems take the form of catalogues or lists. Information is marshaled in service of an overarching category or theme — although the category or theme may not become clear until the end of the poem. Concluding with its argument about America, the unexpectedly capricious "England" begins its catalogue of supposedly essential national qualities with England ("with its baby rivers and little towns, each with its abbey or its cathedral"), but then shifts swiftly to Italy ("with its equal / shores — contriving an epicureanism from which the grossness has been // extracted"), Greece ("with its goats and its gourds, the best of modified illusions"), France ("in / whose products, mystery of construction diverts one from what was originally one's / object — substance at the core"), then finally to America ("in which letters are written / not in Spanish, not in Greek, not in Latin, not in shorthand / but in plain American which cats and dogs can read!").

"There is something attractive about a mind that moves in a straight line," says Moore, describing her own sensibility. Following poems like "England," which surge forward, refusing to circle back, Moore shifts from syllabics to free verse in order to sustain such linear structures in increasingly longer poems: rather than cutting against her syntax, her free-verse lines tend to follow the shapes of the poem's clauses and phrases, foregrounding their repetitions. What are the pressingly Herculean tasks before us?

To popularize the mule . . .
to teach the bard . . .
to prove to the high priests . . .
to teach the patron-saint-to-atheists . . .
to convince snake-charming controversialists . . .

Moore's answer to the question posed by "The Labors of Hercules" is a sequence of parallel infinitive phrases, each beginning a new free-verse line. Her turn to free verse represents not a disavowal of formal patterning but a different kind of patterning — a collusion of line and syntax in poems whose extravagantly list-like organization needs to be managed.

This strategy culminates in the longest poem of *Observations*, "An Octopus," which is no more about a cephalopod than "England" is about a small island nation on the periphery of Europe. The poem grew out of Moore's 1922 expedition to Mount Rainier, the fourteen-thousand-foot peak towering above Seattle, and, as Clifton Johnson puts it in *What to See in America* (one of Moore's sources for the poem), the twenty-eight glaciers covering Mount Rainier, which reach "into rich gardens of wild flowers and splendid evergreen forests like the tentacles of a huge octopus." But just as the octopus is a figure for the mountain, the mountain is Moore's figure for America — its vastness, its multiplicity, its tortured past and its promising future. Except for Whitman's *Leaves of Grass*, there is no poem that more passionately fulfills Emerson's conviction that "America is a poem in our eyes; its ample geography dazzles the imagination."

The poem itself must be experienced in its vastness. Quotation can't reveal the power of Moore's exquisite control of the poem's almost unwieldy array of materials, for its argument emerges through the excessive iterations of catalogue, managed by the lineation, rather than from the logical procedures of cause and effect. Grippingly meticulous accounts of Mount Rainier's geography, fauna, and flora, much of the material quoted from a bewildering variety of sources, ultimately spill into a charged comparison between this "American 'menagerie of styles'" and the ancient Greek preference for mere "neatness of finish." The Greeks wore themselves out, gorgeously so, but this new-world poem, like the glaciers of Mount Rainier, keeps expanding, building a concatenation of materials that feels simultaneously inevitable and impossible — "An Octopus / of ice" distinguished by a relentless "capacity for fact." How, one wants to ask when reading *Observations* from start to finish, could the book have come to this? Read as a whole, as it was designed to be, *Observations* emerges as one of several books that in the 1920s created our lasting sense of what constitutes the modernist achievement — books that court chaos through exquisite artistry: Eliot's *The Waste Land*, Pound's *A Draft of XVI Cantos*, Joyce's *Ulysses*.

How would such a book conclude? "The Octopus" is followed in *Observations* by one last poem, "Sea Unicorns and Land Unicorns," but even this poem doesn't get the last word, whatever that could be.

white, nine kinds
wife, a coffin
Wilcox, W. D.
Will Honeycomb
willows at Oxford
Wilson, V. A.

Xenophon
x-ray

Yawman-Erbe
Yeats, W. B.
Yellow

zebras

Observations concludes with an index, an index in which Moore catalogues not only the titles of her poems but their astonishing arrays of references, from zebras to Xenophon to the phrase "a wife is a coffin" (attributed to Ezra Pound). Following on the explosively centripetal energies of the book's concluding poems, the index feels like the long poem in which *Observations* was meant to conclude, a poem at once errant and composed, perfectly logical yet unrelievedly strange.

In a sense, this combination of qualities distinguishes any great poem, which will seem seductively unpredictable to the degree that it is exquisitely constructed. No poet is more formally precise than Whitman at his most expansive; no poet is more wildly extravagant than Emily Dickinson at her most curtailed. Freedom is not sloppiness, structure is not constriction. But more clearly than almost any other poet of the twentieth century, Moore allows us to see why this is the case. Hence her extraordinary usefulness for other poets, hence her lasting influence on poets who do not sound like her, much less transform her discoveries into methods or mannerisms. Whatever has happened in American poetry over the last hundred years, no poems have become more extravagant, more meticulous, more pick-your-adjective than Marianne Moore's.

II

Home Thoughts

Ezra Pound was born in Hailey, Idaho, in 1885; he died in Venice, Italy, in 1972. In between, he lived for extended periods of time in London, Paris, and the Ligurian resort town of Rapallo: each of these places he left with a feeling of having failed. Though Pound is at heart a lyric poet, his lifelong ambition was (as he told his mother as a very young man) to write the epic of the West. The *Cantos*, left unfinished at Pound's death, is a record of the various forms this ambition would take. But this difficult, exasperating, beautiful poem was only one component of Pound's larger ambition, which was to rejuvenate Western culture — to make available to Western culture the full panoply of its neglected or unappreciated riches. The romantic poet Percy Shelley said famously that poets were the unacknowledged legislators of their time; Pound said they ought to be acknowledged legislators.

There is something narcissistic but also something noble about this ambition: it forced Pound to think of himself as someone stuck in a world that refused to acknowledge his power to make that world a better place — someone eternally exiled from the cultural richness to which he also aspired. One by one, every place Pound lived disappointed him by refusing his efforts to transform that place into the cultural capital it deserved to be.

so that leaving America I brought with me $80
    and England a letter of Thomas Hardy's
    and Italy one eucalyptus pip

In these lines from the *Pisan Cantos*, written at the end of the Second World War when Pound was incarcerated at the Disciplinary Training Center near Pisa, Pound looks back most immediately to the moment when he was apprehended by Italian partisans and turned over to the United States government, which had indicted him for treason because of radio broadcasts in which he'd supported Mussolini's fascist government: leaving his house in the hills above Rapallo, Pound plucked a eucalyptus pip from a tree growing along the path.

But despite the extraordinary circumstances surrounding this moment, Pound connects it to earlier occasions in which he was (in his own mind) similarly forced to emigrate. After having lived in London for a decade, Pound left that city for good in 1920, his ambition to make London the cultural capital of the world permanently deflated. Twelve years earlier, in 1908, Pound had abandoned the country of his birth with a similarly exasperated sense of America's refusal to inhabit its potential. He had eighty dollars in his pocket because on February 14, 1908, he had been fired from his job as an instructor of romance languages at Wabash College in Crawfordsville, Indiana. From that moment on, Pound lived not in exile but at home. To leave London with a letter by Thomas Hardy was not only like leaving Rapallo with a eucalyptus pip; it was also like leaving Crawfordsville with eighty bucks.

Pound's *Cantos* begin with an act of leaving.

And then went down to the ship,
Set keel to breakers, forth on the godly sea, and
We set up mast and sail on that swart ship,
Bore sheep aboard her, and our bodies also
Heavy with weeping, and winds from sternward
Bore us out onward with bellying canvas.

These opening lines of Canto 1, originally published in 1917, are Pound's English version of a passage from the eleventh book of

Homer's *Odyssey*, a passage Pound suspected was the oldest in Homer. The passage goes on to describe how Odysseus speaks with the spirits of the dead by pouring out a pool of sheep's blood; ghosts who drink from the pool are able to speak with human voices.

Pound wants us to think of this passage as a metaphor for his ambition in the *Cantos*, which he once defined as a "poem including history." The poem is populated by ghosts—the speaking presences of the dead—which Pound brings back to life. Pound's medium is not sheep's blood but language, and Canto 1 asks us to think about the rejuvenating power of language in a particular way. Pound does not translate the passage directly from Homer's Greek; instead, he translates from a Latin translation of Homer's Greek that was made by the sixteenth-century Italian poet Andreas Divus. What's more, rather than translating the Latin translation into modern English, Pound translates it into a sonic approximation of Old English, the eighth-century language of "Beowulf" and "The Seafarer," which is now all but incomprehensible to our ears. In a line like "Bore sheep aboard her, and our bodies also," you can hear Pound emulating the starkly alliterative line of Old English poetry.

Rather than making an unknown passage from Homer familiar to us, Pound is making a familiar passage from Homer alive again. Latin was already a dead language by the time Andreas Divus translated the *Odyssey*; his translation represents the effort of the Renaissance to reconfigure the classical origins of Western culture. By translating Divus's Latin translation into an archaic-sounding version of English, Pound is enacting a renaissance of the Renaissance. Rather than making translation a transparent vehicle, through which we come to know an alien past, Pound wants us to become aware of the process of transmission happening in the present. He wants us not only to remember Homer but also to remember the ways in which we've come to know Homer in our time.

This notion of a renaissance of the Renaissance is crucial to what we've come to think of as Pound's modernism. The phrase "make it new" mattered to Pound because he was talking about the past: in order for culture to progress, the past needed to be made available to us—made strange to us, so that we might inhabit its energies viscerally. "A renaissance is a thing made—a thing made by conscious propaganda," said Pound when he was living in London in 1914.

But just a few years later, when the first cantos were published, Pound was again living in the Crawfordsville state of mind: he already felt that his own effort to forge a renaissance was doomed to fail. Pound published what he called "Three Cantos of a Poem of Some Length" in 1917, and the passage that now stands as Canto 1 (the passage translated from Divus's Latin translation of Homer's Greek) was originally the conclusion of Canto 3. In either position, the passage functions simultaneously as an emblem for and an embodiment of the intricate process of cultural recovery. But in its original position, the Homeric passage appears to be not the point from which we begin but the culmination of a series of efforts to resurrect the energies of the Renaissance for the twentieth century: the passage is preceded by a variety of more discursive accounts of how one might, in dire circumstances, enact a renaissance of the Renaissance.

I knew a man, but where 'twas no matter:
Born on a farm, he hankered after painting;
His father kept him at work;
No luck—he married and got four sons;
Three died, the fourth he sent to Paris—
Ten years of Julian's and the ateliers,
Ten years of life, his pictures in the salons,
Name coming in the press.
                              And when I knew him,
Back once again, in middle Indiana,
Acting as usher in the theatre,
Painting the local drug-shop and soda bars,

The local doctor's fancy for the mantel-piece;
Sheep-jabbing the wool upon their flea-bit backs—
The local doctor's ewe-ish pastoral;
Adoring Puvis, giving his family back
What they had spent for him, talking Italian cities,
Local excellence at Perugia,
                              dreaming his renaissance,
Take my Sordello!

These lines are about Fred Vance and his father George Vance, the two best friends Pound made in Crawfordsville while teaching at Wabash College. George Vance had entertained artistic ambitions, but it was his son Fred who lived them, studying at the Art Institute of Chicago and then at the Académie Julian in Paris. Subsequently he lived in Italy and France, but around the time Pound began teaching at Wabash in the fall of 1907, Fred Vance came home to Crawfordsville. Though he would return to France as a soldier in the First World War, Vance would find employment as a painter at home, decorating the walls of the local Elks Club and, more prominently, a theater in New Orleans and the grill room of the Grant Hotel in San Diego.

"I knew a man," begins Pound's passage about Fred Vance, "but where 'twas no matter." The location doesn't matter not because Crawfordsville does not matter but because the story Pound is about to tell could happen anywhere—Crawfordsville, London, Paris, Rapallo. For what Pound saw in Fred Vance was an image of himself: the artist who sets out to connect himself to the great artistic achievements of Western culture and to extend those achievements, making them new—the artist who ultimately finds himself not at the center of a new renaissance but back in Crawfordsville, adoring the French painter Puvis, speaking of life in the Italian city of Perugia, and dreaming his renaissance rather than living it.

To this artist Pound says, "Take my Sordello!"—by which he means: take my poem. Pound had discussed the thirteenth-century poet Sordello (as well as the Victorian poet Robert Browning's poem about Sordello) earlier in the 1917 cantos, and by handing that act of cultural recovery over to Fred Vance, Pound does two things: he honors Vance's effort to become a great painter; and, more poignantly, he associates Vance's failure to become a great painter with his own sense of immanent failure — his growing sense that everyone who attempts to build a renaissance will find himself in a Crawfordsville of the mind, dreaming of the renaissance he failed to make real. In a sense, Pound's cantos began as an elegy for the doomed effort the poem would nonetheless undertake for the next fifty years.

The story of Pound's five months at Wabash College is well known to his readers, but inevitably more as legend than as fact: the great avant-garde artist was constrained, mistreated, by a narrow, parochial village of the American Midwest, then, once that village expelled him, was liberated to undertake greater things in the great cities of Europe. I don't think this story is right, and I don't think Pound himself thought it was right: the passage from Canto 80 — which equates the eucalyptus pip with a letter from Thomas Hardy and the eighty dollars from Wabash College — tells a different story. And even more viscerally, Pound's tender respect for Fred Vance tells a different story. The painter from Crawfordsville is presented in the early cantos not as a pathetic failure, but a noble failure, an artist who had no choice but to live in exile, dreaming of a renaissance rather than living in it. The fate of Fred Vance is not something from which Pound fled; it was a fate he coveted: it conferred on Pound an identity that would not change much over the next fifty years.

"I am homesick after mine own kind," wrote Pound while he was teaching in Crawfordsville, "And ordinary people touch me not."

> And I am homesick
> After mine own kind that know, and feel
> And have some breath for beauty and the arts.

Aye, I am wistful for my kin of the spirit
And have none about me save in the shadows
When come *they*, surging of power, "DAEMON,"
"Quasi KALOUN." S. T. says Beauty is most that, a
            "calling to the soul."
Well then, so call they, the swirlers out of the mist of my soul,
They that come mewards, bearing old magic.

But for all that, I am homesick after mine own kind
And would meet kindred even as I am,
Flesh-shrouded bearing the secret.

The "S. T." to whom Pound refers in this passage from "In Durance" is Samuel Taylor Coleridge. Pound quotes Coleridge's definition of beauty from an essay called "On the Principles of Genial Criticism," a definition derived in turn from Plato: beauty, says Coleridge, is a *"calling on* the soul, which receives instantly, and welcomes it as something connatural." Adapting this sense of beauty in his poem, Pound says that his soul recognizes the spirits of beauty because those spirits emanate from his soul: "the swirlers out of the mist of my soul" come "mewards, bearing old magic." But while this logic ought to render him perfectly self-satisfying, Pound feels exiled rather than complete. He wants to know not just spiritual emanations but "flesh-shrouded" souls, real people: "I am homesick / After mine own kind," Pound repeats, "that know, and feel / And have some breath for beauty and the arts." These lines might make Crawfordsville sound like the barren outpost of the legend, but where in this logic is the home for which Pound is sick? What would it mean for the author of these lines to be fully at home in the present, satisfied with the world as it is now?

When Pound left the United States with eighty bucks in 1908, he headed to Venice, the city where, more than any other place on earth, the past is inextricably and palpably woven into the texture of everyday life. Nothing in Venice is indigenous; everything is borrowed or pillaged or adapted from some other place and time. The great Victorian critic John Ruskin, from whom Pound learned a great deal, maintained that, unlike other Italian cities, Venice didn't really need the Renaissance because it had never ceased to be infused by Arab and Byzantine cultures that had themselves rejuvenated the classical origins of Western culture in multiple ways. This is true of the great instances of Venetian painting or architecture, but it's also true of what you might think of as any ordinary house on any ordinary Venetian canal: the very stones have history—as if the city were a living version of the kind of culturally layered poem Pound tried to make in the Homeric passage from the early cantos.

No wonder, then, that Pound could not stay in Venice: there was no possibility of deprivation there, no need to rekindle the energies of the Renaissance, no reason to write the kind of poems Pound was writing. By saying of his time in Crawfordsville that he was homesick after his kind, Pound was describing the state of mind that he required—a state of mind that he would replicate in London and Paris, cities that, whatever their riches, enabled Pound's work as cultural instigator as Venice did not. Pound left Venice after five months, saying he wanted to head up to London in order to meet William Butler Yeats—the poet whom Pound would soon describe as "a specialist in renaissances." Pound aspired to that position himself, and the aspiration required a town in which he would by definition feel homesick for a home that did not yet exist.

Yeats seemed to Pound a specialist in renaissances because of Yeats's work with other artists in the Irish Renaissance, an effort to resurrect and capitalize upon Ireland's cultural heritage in ways that would give the Irish people not only cultural but also political prominence. Many people thought of Yeats this way; the African American writers of what came to be known as the Harlem Renaissance also looked to Yeats, specialist in renaissances, as a model for their work. But unlike them, Pound also craved the proximity of Yeats's prestige, and after arriving in

London he quickly became part of Yeats's inner circle, eventually developing with Yeats a friendship whose intimacy excluded the circle, in part because Pound and Yeats would marry women who were best friends.

But if you'd imagine that such an alliance, with the man whom Pound thought of as the greatest living poet, would make Pound feel at home, you'd be wrong. Pound's greatest achievement during the London years was his engineering of the Imagist movement, an avant-garde push for a lyric poetry of intense precision and immediacy, but in most of the Imagist poems Pound writes not of a feeling of camaraderie within that avant-garde movement but about the shallowness of village life and his longing for flesh-shrouded companions.

Come my cantilations,
Let us dump our hatreds into one bunch and be done with them,
Hot sun, clear water, fresh wind,
Let me be free of pavements,
Let me be free of printers.
Let come beautiful people
Wearing raw silk of good colour,
Let come graceful speakers,
Let come the ready of wit,
Let come the gay of manner, the insolent and the exulting.
We speak of burnished lakes,
Of dry air, as clear as metal.

This poem, called "Come My Cantilations," is happening now, its imperatives lodged permanently in the present tense. Yet the grammatical mood of its final two lines is deceptive, for the lines should say that we *would* speak of burnished lakes and dry air if only the true companions would appear to rescue us from the doldrums world of pavements and printers. "Come My Cantilations" is a beautifully made poem, subtle and sure-footed in ways that an early apprentice poem like "In Durance" is not, but it makes the same argument about London that the earlier poem made about Crawfordsville. "London is dead to deadish," said Pound when he abandoned the city in 1920. And as Dr. Johnson once said, the man who is tired of London is tired of life. Paris immediately seemed like another Crawfordsville: Picabia and Cocteau "are intelligent," Pound admitted, "which a damn'd number of Parisians aren't." Crawfordsville, London, Paris, Rapallo: Pound lived at home.

Home sounds less interesting, less exotic or challenging than exile, but is it necessarily? There's something pathetic about the artist who never changes, who continually recreates the terms of his own failure so that he might enjoy a strange species of success, and over time this logic isolated Pound from the world he also wanted to change. While living in London, Pound declared that his older friends W. B. Yeats and Ford Madox Ford were the two giants of the English language, and after four decades Pound's feelings had not changed. Incarcerated near the end of the war, he eulogized Ford and Yeats as great artists whom the culture did not appreciate sufficiently, beginning with a line from his own translation of the Old English "Seafarer."

Lordly men are to earth o'ergiven
   these the companions
Fordie that wrote of giants
   and William who dreamed of nobility

Even here, in the Disciplinary Training Center, is the Crawfordsville state of mind, the elegiac sense of foreclosed possibility that honors the renegade artist by making his inevitable failure seem noble. These lines commemorate the artistic community Pound craved, mourned, but finally could not allow himself to experience. The fulfillment of the dream would deprive him of purpose, and the true community—one that included Fred Vance as much as W. B. Yeats—could not be found anywhere on earth.

III

Visions and Revisions

T. S. Eliot had five mothers, or perhaps six. Growing up in St. Louis, Missouri, he was supervised not only by his mother and four older sisters (the eldest of whom was nineteen years his senior), but also by his maternal grandmother, who lived next door. Abigail Adams Eliot had herself grown up in Washington, DC, and could recall clearly her great-uncle, the second president of the United States, after whose wife she had been named.

Great things were expected of the youngest Eliot, and a crucial part of his genius was to have achieved greatness in forms that no one in his family was fully equipped to countenance. Simultaneously, he fulfilled and decimated their expectations, constructing a life that allowed his family to admire his achievement only inasmuch as they were also bewildered, incapable of helping themselves to the side dish of self-congratulation that usually accompanies the main course of parental pride. The author of *The Waste Land* and *Four Quartets* secured the loyalty of his admirers (as well as the unshakable attention of his detractors) in precisely the same way.

"As a scholar his rank is high," wrote Charlotte Eliot of her sixteen-year-old son to the headmaster of Milton Academy, "but he has been growing rapidly, and for the sake of his physical well being we have felt that it might be better for him to wait a year before entering on his college career." Eliot had already been accepted at Harvard College, but his mother preferred that he endure another year of preparatory school. At Milton Academy, in

Massachusetts, he was infantilized because of his frailty, the only boy forbidden to play football or swim in a nearby quarry pond, but at the same time he was expected to reflect his family's ambitions with achievements of immense precocity. Only a few years later, when Eliot began to buck the family's notions of what constituted achievement, declining to defend his doctoral dissertation in philosophy, his mother would show that she understood the newly professionalized world of higher education as well as she understood the dangers of quarry ponds: "The Ph.D. is becoming in America, and presumably also in England, almost an essential for an Academic position and promotion therein. The male teachers in our secondary schools are as a rule inferior to the women teachers, and they have little social position or distinction." Eliot, who was by this time already living in England, did not return to Harvard to receive his degree, despite having written a dissertation that the philosopher Josiah Royce declared the work of an expert, and despite Harvard's philosophy department's having made it clear that a position in its ranks awaited him.

Instead, in 1915, Eliot married Vivien Haigh-Wood only two months after having met her, and embarked on a precarious career as a poet and journalist, supplementing this work first with teaching at High Wycombe Grammar School and later with a full-time position in the Colonial and Foreign Department of Lloyds Bank, where he would help settle the financial fate of Europe in the aftermath of the First World War. In 1920, Eliot published *The Sacred Wood*, a work of literary criticism so influential in both England and the United States (where it became the foundation of the New Criticism) that he created the taste by which he himself was judged for the next fifty years. Then, in 1922, he published a long poem on which he had been working for some years, at first intermittently and, finally, after a breakdown in 1921, with great fervor. "To her the marriage brought no happiness," remembered Eliot of his first wife. "To me, it brought the state of mind out of which came *The Waste Land*."

The marriage was crucial to Eliot's life and work, but not precisely in the way this theatrically grim comment suggests. Both Eliots were chronically ill, often despondent, and their hypochondria was mutually reinforcing; their letters are brimming with long rehearsals of their physical complaints, and, as one might expect, most of the complaints were aimed at Eliot's mother, whom Eliot entreated repeatedly to visit: "If I were dangerously ill I believe you would come no matter how inconvenient." But Charlotte Eliot alternately ignored and parried her son's entreaties, so much so that Eliot was driven to examine her behavior with the intensity that distinguishes all his writing. "It is almost impossible for any of our family to make up their minds," he confessed to his brother. If their mother could "look ahead and not see, in the Eliot way, only the immediate difficulties and details, she would make up her mind at once and come this summer."

The Eliot Way—a compulsion to drive oneself to inaction through the meticulous weighing of alternatives—was something Eliot himself knew all too well. In an essay about Henry Adams, the late nineteenth-century man of letters to whom Eliot was distantly related (Adams having been the great-grandson of the second president of the United States), he referred to the Eliot Way more generally as the Boston Doubt, "a scepticism which is difficult to explain to those who are not born to it." Eliot's ancestor Andrew Eliot had settled in Massachusetts around 1670, and there the family remained until William Greenleaf Eliot, Eliot's grandfather, moved to St. Louis to establish the first Unitarian church west of the Mississippi. "This scepticism," Eliot went on, "is a product, or a cause, or a concomitant, of Unitarianism." Wherever someone infected with the Eliot Way stepped, "the ground did not simply give way, it flew into particles." Such people "want to do something great," said Eliot, but "they are predestined failures."

Eliot's first great artistic success grew from an effort to distance himself from the threat of such failure by dramatizing

it, making us feel it happening as the poem unfolds. Not only
the voice but the very linguistic texture of "The Love Song of
J. Alfred Prufrock" embodies the typically Eliotic stalemate between fortitude and inertia ("There will be time ... yet for a hundred indecisions, / And for a hundred visions and revisions, /
Before the taking of a toast and tea"), the sonorous, incantatory
rhyming of the words *indecisions, visions,* and *revisions* upbraided
by the fussily alliterative monosyllables of *toast* and *tea.* Subsequently, the condition of being paralyzed by a multiplicity of
possible feelings became the emotional core of *The Waste Land,*
the long poem in which the Eliot Way repeatedly thwarts erotic
promise.

"You gave me hyacinths first a year ago;
"They called me the hyacinth girl."
— Yet when we came back, late, from the Hyacinth garden,
Your arms full, and your hair wet, I could not
Speak, and my eyes failed, I was neither
Living nor dead, and I knew nothing.

Yet however arresting in themselves, passages such as these do
not represent the whole of Eliot's sensibility, for throughout *The
Waste Land,* as throughout the life, the Eliot Way is counter-
manded by a willed decisiveness, a determination to act that is
nurtured so privately that to anyone else it appears irrational:
"the awful daring of a moment's surrender / Which an age of pru-
dence can never retract."

    Eliot's marriage to Vivien is the result of such a moment, as
would be his subsequent decisions (often inexplicable even to
the people who knew him best) to enter the Church of England
or, many years later, to marry his secretary, Valerie Fletcher.
The only way he could release himself from the clutches of six
mothers — from his own clutches — was to do something utterly
unprecedented and irrevocable. The mere decision to pursue a
literary life in England would not have lasted; any such decision

could have been reconsidered, modified, delayed. But to link his life inexorably to Vivien's was to preempt all subsequent visions and revisions, allowing the boy from St. Louis to become the author of *The Sacred Wood* and *The Waste Land*. The marriage was torture, but I suspect that for Eliot it relieved him from what he already knew would be worse, a life shaped merely by the Eliot Way. "The present year has been, in some respects, the most awful nightmare of anxiety that the mind of man could conceive," he wrote to his brother in 1916, "but at least it is not dull."

Eliot's poems, though they contain some of the most gripping dramatizations of boredom in the language, are never dull; his letters, which have only recently begun to be collected, are sometimes boring to a degree that can hardly be borne — though revealingly so. After publishing *The Waste Land* in 1922, Eliot settled into his work at the bank and at *The Criterion*, the literary magazine he founded and edited, with an avidity for indecisions and decisions that makes his mother's affliction with the Eliot Way seem insignificant. "I enclose two more articles for No. 3," he wrote to Richard Cobden-Sanderson, the magazine's publisher. "This is nearly everything; there will certainly be one more if not two but not more than two; one possibly from myself. I should like to know the number of words in each contribution as soon as possible."

Yet these letters are also weirdly gripping because one never knows when one might be stopped dead by a letter of singular importance, a letter in which the Eliot Way is superseded by the awful daring of a moment's surrender.

I have made myself into a *machine*. I have done it deliberately — in order to endure, in order not to feel — *but it has killed V*. . . . I have deliberately killed my senses — I have deliberately died — in order to go on with the outward form of living — This I did in 1915. . . . But the dilemma — to kill another person by being dead, or to kill them by being alive? Is it best to make oneself a machine, and kill them by not giving nourishment, or to be alive, and kill them by wanting something that one *cannot* get from that person? Does it happen that two persons' lives are absolutely hostile? Is it true that sometimes one can only live by another's dying? . . . Must I kill her or kill myself? I have *tried* to kill myself—but only to make the machine which kills her. . . . Does she want to die? Can I save myself and her by recognizing that she is more important than I?

This letter, written to the critic John Middleton Murry in the spring of 1925, may seem to confirm handy and long-standing notions about the poet who said in his most famous essay, "Tradition and the Individual Talent," that poetry "is not a turning loose of emotion, but an escape from emotion." But Eliot was no mere manipulator of masks, and this letter does not represent anything so simple as a dropping of his guard. Like his poems, his letters vacillate between the life-deadening equivocations of the Eliot Way and the life-determining thrill of a moment's surrender to decisive action, and the latter impulse is rendered powerful by the former, not occluded by it. "Of course," added Eliot in "Tradition and the Individual Talent," "only those who have personality and emotions know what it means to want to escape from these things."

Eliot was not literally violent, but psychic life seemed to him essentially violent; he believed that by existing he couldn't help but to harm his wife, either by continuing to live with her (the Eliot Way) or by abandoning her for a new life (the awful daring). This dilemma is not confined to one letter but reoccurs throughout Eliot's work, most prominently in *The Family Reunion*, his finest play, in which the protagonist suffers from the horrible, guilt-ridden illusion that he has indeed killed his wife. It also glimmers in the jazzy dialogue of his fragmentary drama *Sweeney Agonistes*—

I knew a man once did a girl in
Any man might do a girl in
Any man has to, needs to, wants to
Once in a lifetime, do a girl in

— and, so far as I know, is first dramatized in "Eeldrop and Appleplex," a curious short story Eliot published in 1917.

> In Gopsum Street a man murders his mistress. The impor-
> tant fact is that for the man the act is eternal, and that for the
> brief space he has to live, he is already dead. He is already
> in a different world from ours. He has crossed the frontier.
> The important fact that something is done which cannot be
> undone — a possibility which none of us realize until we face
> it ourselves. For the man's neighbors the important fact is
> what the man killed her with? And at precisely what time?
> And who found the body? . . . But the medieval world, in-
> sisting on the eternity of punishment, expressed something
> nearer the truth.

This is Eliot's most articulate account of the moment of awful
daring — the irrevocable action, in this case literally violent,
that obliterates the Eliot Way. The aftermath of the action, an
otherwise unavailable sense of damnation, crystallizes the actor,
making him seem horrifying to himself if not to other people,
who go on perceiving him through more readily available cate-
gories of knowledge. Shortly after writing "Eeldrop and Appleplex," Eliot went on a walking tour of southern France with Ezra
Pound, and at a castle near Excideuil (as Pound would remember the incident in Canto 29) he suddenly turned to Pound
and blurted, "I am afraid of the life after death," and then, after
a pause, "Now, at last, I have shocked him." Eliot had already
crossed the frontier, living publicly in the inane doldrums of the
Eliot Way but privately in a medieval world of sin, guilt, and eter-
nal punishment.

Judging from the evidence of his letters alone, Eliot would seem to have been one of the most unhappy people who has ever lived. But the tensions that had always characterized his sensibility, inflated from Prufrock's drawing room to an eschatological arena of Dantean proportions, continued to fuel his best work even at the most unhappy times. Almost immediately after completing *The Waste Land,* he confessed that the poem seemed to him "a thing of the past" and that he was "feeling toward a new form and style." What he wanted was a way of representing in language what could not be represented at all—the inner life of a person beyond the frontier, a person doomed to be recognizable to other people when in fact he is already dead—and the result was "The Hollow Men," the poetic sequence with which he struggled, trying out a variety of drafts and rearrangements, between 1922 and 1925, when it appeared as the final poem in *Poems, 1909–1925.*

Audible here are the familiar equivocations of the Eliot Way—

Between the desire
And the spasm
Between the potency
And the existence
Between the essence
And the descent
Falls the Shadow

—but in contrast to "Prufrock" or *The Waste Land,* Eliot's language has become severely chastened, apparently more oracular than spoken, as if the poem were attempting to give the impression of being uttered from a space beyond language, the space of the dead, the damned, a space in which the everyday marks of human individuality have fallen away. Inexpiable guilt drives the sequence, nowhere more poignantly than in these lines, which Eliot published in two preliminary versions of "The Hollow Men" but ultimately cut from the final version.

This is my affliction
Eyes I shall not see again
Eyes of decision
Eyes I shall not see unless
At the door of death's other kingdom
Where, as in this,
The eyes outlast a little while
A little while outlast the tears
And hold us in derision.

Nowhere in "The Hollow Men" does Eliot make reference to the everyday world in which people drink tea, work at banks, write letters, torture their wives, but the presence of Vivien Eliot, the woman though whom Eliot constructed his life as a poet, hovers over every line. "I am sorry I tortured you and drove you mad," wrote Vivien from a nursing home in 1925. "I had no notion until yesterday afternoon that I had done it. I have been simply raving mad."

"The Hollow Men" remains a confounding performance, at once viscerally immediate and strangely abstracted, resistant to description in a way that the achievements that precede and follow it, *The Waste Land* and *Four Quartets*, whatever their difficulties, are not. But perhaps for this very reason, the poem seems to me the most quintessentially Eliotic of all the poet's performances, at once excessive and curtailed, irresistibly charismatic yet forever elusive, its power immediately apparent yet very difficult to describe. In a sense, the poem does feel impersonal — not because it is unemotional (far from it) but because it gives voice to emotions too primal for words, emotions unmarked by the surface trappings of the merely personal. This quality is, I suspect, what fuels the impression, even a century after the publication of his early masterpieces, that Eliot is an inordinately difficult writer: nothing is ever hidden, but neither is anything plain.

Nor could it be otherwise. Not only Eliot's poems but also his essays and letters are driven by this logic, and once one becomes

aware of the constant battle waged between the awful daring and
the Eliot Way, Eliot's demeanor seems less surreptitious than inevitable. Famously, he maintained in "Tradition and the Individual Talent" that the past is "altered by the present as much
as the present is directed by the past," and in an introduction to
an obscure historical poem called *Savonarola*, published around
the same time as "The Hollow Men," he offers more extended
remarks about the relativity of historical interpretation; but nowhere in this introduction does he acknowledge that the author
of *Savonarola* is his mother, Charlotte Eliot, who at the age of
eighty-three was publishing her first book of poems.

> The role played by interpretation has often been neglected in
> the theory of knowledge. Even Kant, devoting a lifetime to
> the pursuit of categories, fixed only those which he believed,
> rightly or wrongly, to be permanent. . . . Some years ago, in
> a paper on *The Interpretation of Primitive Ritual*, I made an
> humble attempt to show that in many cases *no* interpretation
> of a rite could explain its origin.

Reaching back to his abandoned work in the Harvard philosophy department, these sentences constitute one of Eliot's most
deeply felt exchanges with his mother. They are a gift to the
woman who, when he threw over an academic career in favor
of poetry, admitted with heartbreakingly misplaced confidence
that "I have absolute faith in his Philosophy but not in the *vers
libres.*"

IV

Drawing a Frame

The first line of Gertrude Stein's "Susie Asado" is made of three consonants and one vowel sound: "Sweet, sweet, sweet, sweet, sweet tea." The musical phrase to which Virgil Thomson set this line in 1926, thirteen years after Stein wrote it, consists of two notes, C and E flat: after five terse repetitions of the word "sweet" on C, the singer jumps up a minor third to E flat on "tea." Then the piano enters with a C minor triad. As the song continues, the function of its diction becoming increasingly estranged from the function of its syntax—

Sweet sweet sweet sweet sweet tea.
   Susie Asado.
Susie Asado which is a told tray sure.
A lean on the shoe this means slips slips hers.
When the ancient light grey is clean it is yellow, it is a silver seller.

—the setting's commitment to the simplest harmonic vocabulary hardly wavers: the C minor triad is followed by a C minor scale, played in parallel sevenths, and from then on the accompaniment alternates between triads and scales.

Stein's readers have long debated the meaning of "Susie Asado," but Thomson admitted that he was attracted to Stein's writing precisely because he didn't know what it meant. Treating the text as pure sound, Thomson makes it feel paradoxically more meaningful in the musical setting than it feels on the page.

As Aaron Copland said of Stein's and Thomson's celebrated opera *Four Saints in Three Acts* (1934), Thomson's music draws a frame around Stein's language, the frame consisting of egregiously basic musical gestures.

Since the Renaissance, triads and scales have been the basic building blocks of tonal music — music we can describe as being in a key, such as C minor. When early twentieth-century composers like Arnold Schoenberg set out to compose music not in a key, allowing us to experience dissonance as something that wouldn't require resolution, the basic buildings blocks of tonal music needed to be shunned. But while Thomson foregrounds triads and scales relentlessly in "Susie Asado," as if to suggest a rousing reinvigoration of tonal practice, his repetition of these building blocks never establishes a strong sense of a key: because there's nothing in tension with them, there's nothing at stake in returning to them. Like other American artists who in various ways embraced a disarming simplicity of means (such as Stein), Thomson made familiar artistic gestures seem provocatively strange, and it's misleading to think of him as someone who reacted against the groundbreaking complexities of musical modernism, just as it's misleading to think of Schoenberg's modernism as a reaction against Brahms. Thomson was investigating the range of possibilities inherent in his medium — the medium being, in this case, the notes of the diatonic scale.

For a long time that was hard for some people to hear. Compared with T. S. Eliot's poems, Stein's could seem uninvolved in the great dilemmas of modern culture, and Thomson's music could seem similarly to shun the big questions. Theodor Adorno championed Schoenberg's music because of "the expression of suffering and the pleasure taken in dissonance," a pleasure that was "inextricably interwoven in authentic works of art in the modern age." By comparison, even Igor Stravinsky, whom Adorno dismissed as "the yea-sayer of music," seemed insufficiently serious. In such a climate of taste, a climate that equated anxiety and complexity with authenticity, Thomson's music was

doomed to seem quaint. With the rise in the 1960s of the musical minimalism associated with composers such as Steve Reich,
Thomson began to seem more hip, but this version of postmod-
ernism already seems as blinkered as Adorno's polemical modernism, as Thomson's best music does not.

"There is no Modern spirit. There are only some modern tech-
niques," wrote Thomson in his first book of prose, *The State of
Music* (1939), a book that, along with Kenneth Burke's *Counter-
Statement* (1931), seems to me one of our most incisive accounts
of the production and reception of art in a social setting. It's not
coincidental that these books were published in the 1930s, the
decade that asked many artists of Thomson's and Burke's gen-
eration to consider the modernist achievements of the 1920s in a
new economic and political landscape. But as Thomson's shrewd
comment suggests, he was suspicious of any notion of a modern
sensibility that guided artistic production at large, and, unlike
Adorno, he was especially suspicious of the association of any
sensibility with any particular style of music, painting, or poetry.
If there really were a modern spirit, he mused, then "the market
prices of music and painting and poetry would not be so disparate as they are."

Throughout *The State of Music*, Thomson stresses that artists
are members of a profession: they acquire training, they practice their skills, they get paid. There's nothing dreary about this
demystifying perspective, however, for Thomson is throughout *The State of Music* a beguilingly deadpan manipulator of his
medium—the medium being, in this case, not the notes of the
scale but the syntax and diction of the English language.

"Let me sum up by repeating," concludes the third chapter,
which actually goes on to say something new.

> That music is an island, like Ceylon or Tahiti, or perhaps even
> more like England, which Bossuet called "the most famous
> island in the world." That the waters around it are teeming

with digestible fish that travel in schools and are known as painters. That swimming around among these at high speed and spouting as they go are prehistoric monsters called poets, who terrify all living things, fish and islanders alike. That these monsters are quite tame, however, in spite of their furious airs, and that since they have no industrial value just now, and since their presence offers no real danger to musical life or to the fishing industry (for they attack only one another), they are allowed to survive and are occasionally given food. Indeed, their evolution offers a spectacle that is considered by the islanders to be not only picturesque but salutary, instructive, and grand.

Behind these metaphors lies Thomson's hard-won intimacy with both musical and literary mediums: to learn about counterpoint and harmony, you need to study with someone who is conversant with the composition of music, but to learn about diction and syntax, you don't need necessarily to study with a poet, which is why people who happily send their kids to piano lessons may wonder if poetry can be taught at all. Now that the proliferation of MFA programs in poetry has coincided with the waning of print culture, poets may seem more than ever like harmless prehistoric monsters.

Musicians seem more obviously to be members of a profession. Because an aspiring composer needs to be in close contact with practicing experts, Thomson reasoned, most music is written in great centers of musical activity, while poetry may flourish in isolation. By the same reasoning, a "collaborative" art, such as music or theater, requires the response of critics, as "solitary" arts, such as poetry, may not: "It used to amuse me in Spain that it should take three children to play bull-fight. One plays bull and another plays toreador, while the third stands on the side-lines and cries 'olé!' Music is like that. It takes three people to make music properly, one man to write it, another to play it, and a third to criticize it. Anything else is just a rehearsal." Criticism of the solitary arts is, of course, possible, but Thomson believed that in the collaborative arts criticism is part of the process.

Virgil Garnett Gaines Thomson was born not in a great center of musical activity but in Kansas City, Missouri, in 1896. Like lots of kids, he received piano lessons, but unlike most he was lucky enough to have his musical gifts recognized by a series of dedicated teachers, and by the age of fifteen he was working as a piano accompanist and church organist. After graduating from high school, the 130-pound Thomson enlisted in the National Guard, but the First World War ended before he could be deployed. Then, like those other Missouri modernists, T. S. Eliot and Marianne Moore, Thomson headed east for college, where at Harvard College he studied composition while also continuing to work as an accompanist and organist. At the same time, a young English instructor named S. Foster Damon, who would become an influential Blake scholar, introduced Thomson to the poetry of Gertrude Stein and the music of Erik Satie.

Thomson discovered himself in the whimsically deadpan sensibilities of these two artists, and in 1921 he traveled to Paris to begin studying at the American Conservatory with the legendary teacher Nadia Boulanger, whose students also included Aaron Copland and Elliott Carter. After returning to Harvard to complete his degree, he moved back to Paris, where he would meet not only Stein and Satie but also Jean Cocteau, James Joyce, and Pablo Picasso. "Like Harvard men" was Thomson's way of describing how he and Stein got along, and on January 1, 1927, he played and sang for her his setting of "Susie Asado."

By June, Stein had completed her libretto to *Four Saints in Three Acts*, and Thomson spent the next year or more setting the text (every word of it, including the stage directions) to melodies influenced by American hymn tunes and spirituals. *Four Saints in Three Acts* feels like a happy marriage of Dadaism and Andrew Wyeth: the opera was premiered in 1934 at the Wadsworth Athenaeum in Hartford, Connecticut, with an African-American cast and a set constructed of cellophane, and after selling out its two-week run, it moved to Broadway. Thomson would be famous for the rest of his long life, as both a composer and a writer. After publishing *The State of Music* in 1939, Thomson accepted an invitation to become the chief music critic at the *New York Herald Tribune*, a position he would hold for the next fourteen years. He held court in his apartment in the Chelsea Hotel until his death in 1989.

As Thomson described it, his mission as a reviewer was "to expose the philanthropic persons in control of our institutions for the amateurs they mostly are, to reveal the manipulators of our musical distribution for the culturally retarded profit-makers that indeed they are, and to support with all the power of my praise every artist, composer, group, or impresario whose relation to music is straightforward, by which I mean based only on music and the sound it makes." This is the position staked out by argument, rather than occasion, in *The State of Music*—that our musical life should be guided by artists, not by people who happen to have money. Nobody expects to comprehend astrophysics because they remember their multiplication tables, but people who can't read music may expect to comprehend a new piece of music after hearing it once. Especially in the early twenty-first century, when social media asks us to evaluate a film or a book instantly upon our experience of it, Thomson's call for "slowness of judgment" feels salutary. "A vote seems to be required, a yes or no," he laments, and "persons who cannot follow music at all do well to admit the fact and let music alone."

Thomson had little time for opinionated patrons, flamboyant conductors, or fatuously crowd-pleasing repertoire, and yet the financial health of musical institutions often rides on the rails of such patrons, conductors, repertoire. The problem (to extend Thomson's bullfighting metaphor) is that music requires not only a bull, a toreador, and a discerning observer who cries *olé*; it also requires an arena full of people who buy tickets. Once, when James Joyce was imagining a lucrative career in the theater, his friend Ezra Pound cautioned that there had to be something fundamentally intractable about an art form that requires a thousand people huddled in the dark, night after night, to pay the bills. The remark seems both astute and impatient, and Thomson the reviewer often finds himself similarly caught in a place where his innate Midwestern populism rubs against his equally unaffected Parisian modernism, despite the convincing marriage of these qualities in his own music.

As a critic, Thomson is consequently most engaging when the occasion at hand permits his attention to be diverted from money-making venues ("chamber music in a hall that seats 1,500 people is, of course, a contradiction in terms"), conductors ("the effect on this listener was about what it would be if Orson Welles were to apply his invasion-from-Mars technique to the recounting of a bedtime story"), or performers ("he is authoritative, direct, and courteous, like the captain of a transatlantic liner"), allowing him more purely to describe the experience of listening to the sounds that music makes.

> The closer the performing conditions for Sebastian Bach's concerted music are approximated to those of early eighteenth-century provincial Germany the more the music sounds like twentieth-century American swing. The exactitude with which a minimum time unit is kept unaltered at all times, the persistence of this unit as one of exactly measured length rather than of pulsation, the omnipresence of the harpsichord's ping, like a brush on a cymbal, the constant employment of wiggly counterpoint and staccato bass, all make it a matter of preference between anachronisms whether one puts it that Bach has gone to town or that some of the more scholarly jiggerbugs of the town have wandered into a church.

This passage suggests that the most important unit of composition for Thomson the writer is not so much the sentence as the paragraph. Such passages have a structural integrity that makes their conclusions feel simultaneously inevitable and unpredictable; like lyric poems, they feel like they're being formulated in the time it takes to read them, as the syntax unfolds on the page. Thomson describes musical form not as a static thing but as a "progress," something that asserts its integrity over time, and his best paragraphs feel crafted similarly as temporal events.

Most of those paragraphs are to be found in either *The State of Music* or *The Music Scene*, which brings together the earlier *Herald Tribune* pieces written from 1940 to 1944. Over time, the challenge of producing several reviews each week made Thomson's prose increasingly predictable, the dramatic energy of the well-modulated paragraph giving way to a more serviceable accumulation of remarks. It's difficult to imagine the Thomson of *The State of Music* committing himself to these sentences, in which he looks back on the first fifty years of the twentieth century.

> The world situation of music has altered in every detail, and in most cases there has been a loss of distinction. Even the audience, though much larger and, in the provinces, better informed than it was, is less subtle, less intelligent, less sure of itself. As for Sunday articles, they are written nowadays by people like me. In the early years of this century the critical fraternity contained Ernest Newman, a better historian, and Claude Debussy, a better composer.

The self-depreciation feels egregious, the cultural pessimism predictable, alien to the Thomson one has come to know: an artist whose greatest prose is driven by the need to praise art. "There is only a lack of virtue," he announced far more provocatively in 1942, "art being entirely a positive conception."

The later *Tribune* reviews do offer a detailed chronicle of the musical life of New York—the concerts, the operas, the pianists, the singers, week by week, day by day. And even if this chronicle is not written by Debussy, whom nobody disparages for not being

Mozart, it is written not only by a practicing artist but also by an artist capable of describing the most erudite aspects of musical literacy in words (to borrow from another Missouri modernist) that cats and dogs can understand. "Straightforwardness on the concert platform is something rarely encountered except on the part of children and of the very greatest artists," Thomson said of the soprano Kirsten Flagstad, and straightforwardness is the quality that distinguishes Thomson's real achievement in both literary and musical media. Children lose the power of straight-forwardness once they learn to feel embarrassed, and the delight of Thomson's setting of Stein's "Susie Asado" turns on its un-embarrassed embrace of a simplicity that might, in other hands, seem knowingly strategic. Virtually every interpretation of "Susie Asado" seems destined to feel simultaneously clever and wrong, but Thomson's setting of the song feels unassailable.

Randall Jarrell wrote reviews that are still prized for their clever nastiness and poems that are often dismissed for their sen-timentality; people feel embarrassed by them. But it's clear that the real Jarrell comes out in the poems, which are, to my mind, as insufficiently admired as the prose is overpraised; the nasti-ness was a strategy for assuring Jarrell's audience (and himself) that he could run with the big boys. "It has eschewed the impres-sive, the heroic, the oratorical," said Thomson of the music of his mentor Satie.

> It has valued, in consequence, quietude, precision, acuteness
> of auditory observation, gentleness, sincerity and directness
> of statement. Persons who admire these qualities in private
> life are not infrequently embarrassed when they encounter
> them in public places. It is this embarrassment that gives to
> all French music, and to the work of Satie and his neophytes
> in particular, an air of superficiality.

In both his music and his prose, Thomson was willing to seem as if he ought to be embarrassed. He describes Satie's sensibility

first in its own right, then as an emblem of a national charac-
ter, but Thomson's matter-of-fact prose ultimately makes that
sensibility, easily mistaken for superficiality, feel like a universal
benchmark: whether listening to music or reading poems, who
wouldn't choose gentleness, sincerity, and directness over the
heroic and the oratorical?

What about Beethoven, Thomson himself might ask. What
about Wagner or Mahler? What about Milton or Blake or Pound?
Are they insufficiently embarrassed by their own righteousness?
"Music does not deal in general ideas or morality or salvation,"
Thomson opined. "It expresses private sentiments through skill
and sincerity, both of which last are a privilege, a duty, indeed,
of the private citizen, and no monopoly of the prophetically inclined." This is easier to say about art made of the notes of the
scale than about art made of words; words have meanings, and
a great poem might deal in ideas of morality or salvation — or it
might not. But the power of Thomson's remark rests in his conviction that skill is also among the civic responsibilities of the
musician, poet, or person. Whether inclined toward the pro-
phetic or the private, a poem will not keep happening without it.

V

A Test of Poetry

Despite having written some of the most austerely beautiful poems of the twentieth century, George Oppen is known best for not writing at all. After publishing *Discrete Series* in 1934, a book reviewed by Williams and introduced by Pound ("I salute a serious craftsman"), he entered a period of silence that would not conclude until almost thirty years later, when *The Materials* appeared in 1962. Oppen called himself the oldest promising poet in America, but after *Of Being Numerous* appeared in 1968, it won the Pulitzer Prize.

What distinguishes Oppen's silence is not so much its length as its circumstance. Having been born more than two decades later than Stein, Pound, or Moore, Oppen came of age as a poet during the 1930s, when (like Virgil Thomson) he looked back on the modernist achievement of the '20s from the perspective of a social landscape that had changed utterly. The Great Depression did not simply politicize Oppen the poet: having joined the Communist Party in 1935, Oppen organized the Farmers' Union milk strike, made patterns for Grumman Aircraft, landed in Marseilles with the 103rd Antitank Division, received a Purple Heart, moved to Mexico to avoid being called before the House Un-American Activities Committee, built houses, made furniture, and devoted himself uninterruptedly to his wife and daughter. Most poets spend more time not writing than writing, but most poets do not spend their down time working as a labor organizer, even if they consider their poems to be in some way political.

Though a highly political person, Oppen was not inclined toward what we most commonly recognize as political poetry; he considered the rhetoric of many political poems to be "merely excruciating" — though no more so, as he was quick to recognize, than the rhetoric of many political meetings. In the early 1930s, Oppen was associated with the Objectivist movement, a loose association of avant-garde poets that also included Louis Zukofsky, Charles Reznikoff, and Lorine Neidecker. And while his first book, *Discrete Series*, is starkly elliptical, his later work combines Objectivist precision with a lyricism that his more staunchly experimental colleagues disdained.

Miracle of the children   the brilliant
Children   the word
Liquid as woodlands   Children?

When she was a child I read Exodus
To my daughter   'The children of Israel ...'

Pillar of fire
Pillar of cloud

No other poet sounds like this, at once so intelligent and so tender. However adamant his convictions, Oppen's meticulously shaped lines embody a music of deference — an unwillingness to dominate the world by virtue of having understood it. And whatever else he was, the man who wrote these lines was also the child whose mother had shot herself when he was four years old. Her suicide note: "We've been happy — I love you — I worry about the children and school and their clothes — it seems — since I did this and don't know why — that I am not fitted for the business of life." Half a century after his mother's death, Oppen could recite these words from memory.

"I work sometimes for eight hours or so, fiddling with corrections," says Oppen in his daybooks (collections of fragmentary thoughts, observations, quotations that he began keeping when he returned to poetry after his silence). "But sometimes I am so tired in two or three hours of effort that I'm shaken." These undated pages are variously typed and handwritten; scraps of paper are glued on top of other scraps; pages are held together with staples, pipe cleaners, and (on one occasion) a nail hammered into a block of wood. On the next page: "a poem may be devoted to giving clear meaning to one word."

Oppen was, as Pound recognized immediately, a serious craftsman, and in contrast to his painstakingly finished poems, in which every syllable is weighed, every line-ending calibrated, the palimpsest-like pages of the daybooks reveal the painstaking process through which Oppen achieved this quiet authority. "If the poet begins to ask us to accept a system of opinions and attitudes," says Oppen, explaining why Allen Ginsberg's exhortations seem to him unconvincing, "he must manage the task of rigorous thought." And rigorous thought is registered in language that, in the process of its becoming, reveals the flaws of its author's opinions not only in what it says but more tellingly in how it sounds: "If one revises and revises and revises — perhaps weeks and months and years and cannot revise, then there is something wrong with what you are trying to say. The ear knows." True poetry, says Oppen, is written in "a language that tests itself."

I thought I had encountered

Permanence; thought leaped on us in that sea
For in that sea we breathe the open
Miracle

Of place, and speak
If we would rescue
Love to the ice-lit

Upper World a substantial language
Of clarity, and of respect.

Oppen is thinking of Orpheus here, the poet who failed to rescue
his love, the dead Eurydice, and return her to the upper world.
But the victory of these final lines of "A Narrative" inheres not
simply in what they say but in their intricately seductive manner of saying, a manner that, in its studious equivocations, tests
itself, thereby courting the specter of failure.

How does an exquisitely crafted poem, a poem we'd think of
easily as successful, do that? Compare to Oppen's a little poem
by William Carlos Williams called "The World Contracted to a
Recognizable Image."

at the small end of an illness
there was a picture
probably Japanese
which filled my eye

an idiotic picture
except it was all I recognized
the wall lived for me in that picture
I clung to it as a fly

The first four lines divide Williams's syntax into grammatical
units ("there was a picture"), allowing us easily to absorb its
accumulating sense: a simple sentence emerges, much as the
Japanese print came into focus as the ailing poet opens his eyes.
The second quatrain begins by extending that sentence with an
apposition ("an idiotic picture"), but then the sentence stops
short at the end of the second line, interrupted by two startlingly
terse one-line sentences ("the wall lived for me in that picture /
I clung to it as a fly"), sentences in which the poet suddenly describes not the world but himself. There is no fly in the world

of this poem: the fly is a metaphor for the mind, and we hear it buzzing relentlessly in the poem's exquisitely calibrated dance of syntax and line.

Oppen's poems are often said to resemble Williams's, but while the lineation of William's "The World Contracted to a Recognizable Image" preserves the integrity of the various grammatical clauses and phrases ("there was a picture / probably Japanese / which filled my eye"), Oppen's lineation more generally cuts against the grammatical units of his syntax ("we breathe the open / Miracle // Of place, and speak / If we would rescue / Love"), forcing us to inhabit the language primarily not as a recitation of sense-making—

we breathe the open Miracle of place,
And speak if we could rescue Love

—but as a more arduously probing act of making sense.

        we breathe the open
Miracle

Of place, and speak
If we would rescue
Love

To relineate this syntax as I've just done is to produce the sound of finished thought; in contrast, Oppen's lineation makes us hear the poem as an ongoing act of thinking, a bringing forth that feels as arduous as the Orphic recovery the poem describes. There is no hierarchy among these different manners of lineation (as Marianne Moore's vacillations between highly enjambed syllabic verse and mostly end-stopped free verse also suggests); both Williams's and Oppen's poems are lineated in order to sound precisely as they do, not another way. Oppen's

way of lineating his syntax troubles not only his admission of
failure ("I thought I had encountered // Permanence"): it also
marks his highly equivocating account of how he would succeed.

If we were to rescue love, declares the poem's final sentence
when reduced to its simplest form, *we must speak a language of
clarity and respect*. But by separating the verb ("speak") from its
object ("a substantial language / Of clarity, and respect"), inter-
rupting the sentence with a subordinate clause ("if we would rescue / Love to the ice-lit // Upper World"), and further lineating
that clause so that its nouns are consistently cleaved from their
attendant verbs and adjectives, forcing us to move through the
already complex syntax with increasing deliberation—

If we would rescue
Love to the ice-lit

Upper World

—Oppen allows us to feel how difficult, how precarious, the
achievement of this Orphic ambition might be. He thought he
had encountered permanence: he did not, and the actual recovery of it would depend on our speaking a language of clarity
and respect to which we may only aspire.

Did Oppen consider such language political? Capable of con-
sequence? Generally, twentieth-century American poets recognized two strategies by which a poem might register a political
effect: a poem might express a political position thematically,
through its subject matter (think of Ginsberg); or it might embody a position formally, by disrupting aesthetic norms (think
of Stein). Oppen was wary of both strategies, considering them
dangerously untestable, since the premise of their efficacy too
easily becomes their proof: "We must cease to believe in secret
names and unexpected phrases which will burst the world." Without fanfare, Oppen refused the notion that a poet could fulfill his

social responsibilities merely by writing any kind of poem, and neither did this refusal engender any contempt either for poetry or for social obligation.

"Is it more important to produce art or to take political action," he asks in the daybooks.

> Of course I cannot pretend to answer such a question. I could point this out, however, that art and political action are in precise opposition in this regard: that it can always be quite easily shown that political action is going to be valuable; it is difficult to ever prove that political action has been valuable. Whereas art is precisely the opposite case; it seems always impossible to prove that it is going to be valuable, and yet it is always quite clear that the art of the past has been of value to humanity. I offer it only as a suggestion that art lacks in political action, not action. One does what he is most moved to do.

What one is "most moved to do" may take different forms, all of them equivocal; it isn't possible to predict the efficacy of any human action, whether in politics or art. Oppen needed to stop writing poems in order to do what he was most moved to do, but he never imagined that the terms of his own life could be transformed into imperatives about the relationship of politics and art. In his "Statement on Poetics" he insisted that he could only describe "how to write *that* poem"—not "how to write a poem." His sense of the power of any human action (writing, organizing, raising a daughter) was similarly consigned to its occasion.

This refusal of romance often makes Oppen's admirers nervous. Especially for those readers who are prone to believe that writing itself constitutes political action, Oppen's silence can be rankling. So can Oppen's lyricism: the poems are a little too pretty. To such a reader, Oppen's remark that "there are situations which cannot honorably be met by art" is problematic enough; more troubling is Oppen's sense that "some ideas are not politically useful, or useful to the childhood of a daughter"—which is to say that, since we'll never know the ultimate value of our work, writing poems is probably less important than being a good dad. That wisdom may not be very glamorous, but everything Oppen did suggests that he believed it to be true.

The editor of Oppen's daybooks, Stephen Cope, seems embarrassed that Oppen is not more glamorous, and his annotations are geared toward making the kinds of large claims for writing that Oppen avoids. While admitting that it is "highly unlikely" that Oppen knew Theodor Adorno's work, Cope nonetheless claims that Oppen echoes Adorno's contention that "to write poetry after Auschwitz is barbaric." And when Oppen quotes a well-known verse from the Gospels ("The truth shall make us free"), Cope's tendency to add unearned weight to the daybooks is given free rein: "The phrase that Oppen quotes was also used as an ironic slogan by German revisionist historians who wished to deny the Holocaust, as its German formulation—'Warheit macht Frei'—echoes the Nazi Party dictum 'Arbeit macht Frei' ('Work will set you free'). Given the context here, however, it is unlikely that Oppen is referring to the latter usage." Cope wants desperately for Oppen's words to be freighted with world-historical significance, but his wanly associational notes disregard the values most dear to Oppen himself—precision, clarity, respect.

Neither is this manner of reading Oppen unusual. In a potentially eye-popping study of Oppen's FBI file, published in *American Communist History*, Eric Hoffman rightly notes that Oppen and his wife insisted that they never served as spies for the Soviet government. But because Oppen became outraged when an FBI agent asked if he had ever engaged in espionage, Hoffman asks, "is it possible that . . . either of the Oppens or both were working in some way for Soviet intelligence? Was Oppen's tirade the result of his fear that they might be discovered as having been involved in Soviet espionage?" There is no way to answer these questions—except inasmuch as the questions are meant implicitly to answer themselves, conjecture serving simultaneously as evidence. While Hoffman does discover a record of messages sent by an agent named "Oppen," the messages were intercepted while Oppen was in basic training in Louisiana in 1943. Positing that the messages were sent by Oppen's wife Mary, Hoffman wonders if the reference in the interception to Oppen as "he" may be "a typo."

The logic underwriting this argument (because Oppen could have put his writing to political ends, only the most daunting responsibilities could have silenced him) would have offended Oppen himself. "I could not have continued as I was going with my early poems," he says in the daybooks, looking back on his years of poetic silence. "And we devoted ourselves to creating happiness for the three of us, and for a few friends and their children so far as possible." This unwillingness to exaggerate the importance of his actions—an eagerness to honor family life as much as any other social institution—is Oppen's signature, and the signature is most powerfully sonic, a refusal to write above or beyond the occasion of the poem at hand.

Imagine a poem written out of the conviction that there are situations that cannot honorably be met by poetry. A poem written, therefore, in full awareness of the fact that we may not recognize a situation that cannot be met by poetry when we see it, that we have no choice but to write poems that exhibit our limitations, an exhibition that will seem genuine only when we are writing from the height of our strength. "Art [is] as old as civilization," says Oppen in the daybooks. "If one can add one thing to so long a history, one color or shape or tone, one perception to so long a history, that is a great deal to do." Oppen's victories are no less great for being small.

VI

Life after Death

The *Collected Poems* of Robert Lowell opens a window on the life of a great American poet. That this poet is named Frank Bidart does not distract from Lowell's achievement; in fact, the dynamic relationship between the author and editor of this book helps to rescue Lowell from the story of his own life—a story we may already know too well. For if we're not thinking about Lowell's marriages or his breakdowns, we're thinking about the New Criticism and confessional poetry, movements to which Lowell's achievement is inextricably bound. Around the same time that George Oppen called himself the oldest promising poet in America, the young Lowell's face appeared on the cover of *Time* magazine.

Robert Traill Spence Lowell IV was born in 1917 to a Boston family already famous for the poets Amy and James Russell Lowell. Determined simultaneously to buck and embody the tradition, Lowell left Harvard College in 1937, headed south to Vanderbilt, and pitched a tent on the lawn of the New Critic Allen Tate, who would write an introduction to Lowell's first volume of poems, *Land of Unlikeness*, published seven years later. By then, Lowell had converted to Catholicism, spent five months in jail for refusing military induction, and begun to suffer the first symptoms of his manic breakdowns. Also he had written poems whose formal agility seemed to his mentors exemplary. "T. S. Eliot's recent prediction that we should soon see a return to formal and even intricate meters and stanzas was coming true, before he made it," said Tate in his introduction to *Land of Unlikeness*, "in the verse of Robert Lowell." *Lord Weary's Castle*, Lowell's second volume, published in 1946, would win the Pulitzer Prize.

From this point on, Lowell became the poet that literary history seemed to require just as literary history was happening: while the robustly metered and rhymed poems of *Land of Unlikeness* and *Lord Weary's Castle* answered a late-modernist call for a highly formalist poetry, the suddenly intimate, free-verse poems of *Life Studies* (published in 1959) answered a subsequent need to turn against that call, and Lowell's political and psychological struggles seemed to reinforce the authenticity of the poems. The phrase *confessional poetry* was coined by the critic M. L. Rosenthal in a review of *Life Studies*, and immediately the phrase was employed to describe not just Lowell but a movement also including poets as different from one another as Anne Sexton, John Berryman, and Sylvia Plath. Almost as immediately, however, Lowell himself moved on, embarking on an immense, unfinishable sequence of blank-verse sonnets that would preoccupy him for much of the rest of his life.

This was the Lowell that Frank Bidart came to know at Harvard in the mid-1960s. Lowell was an irrepressible reviser of his own poems, both before and after publication ("Sad friend, you cannot change," was Elizabeth Bishop's epitaph for him), and Bidart became an indispensable part of this open-ended process, serving as "both amanuensis and sounding board," as Bidart has put it. This means that Bidart quite literally participated in the act of making many of the sonnets that appeared first in *Notebook 1967–68* and were then reconfigured in *Notebook*, published in 1970, as well as in a variety of later volumes; Lowell's trust in this young Bidart is moving and disarming. This also means that Bidart spoke intimately with Lowell about the composition of many earlier poems, poems that Lowell would periodically revisit and revise.

Bidart is no Boswell, eager to display his attentions to the great man, but no other editor of a major poet has ever been able to make statements like this: "I once said to Lowell that I thought the revisions that he had made in the text of *Life Studies* . . . were great improvements, especially the punctuation." It's as if Pound, having spent three years poring over punctuation with Yeats at Stone Cottage, had the opportunity to edit the poet from whom he learned everything.

"It is myself that I remake," said Yeats, another inveterate reviser, to readers who missed the earlier versions of poems they'd come to love. Lowell would have agreed, but what is remarkable about him is the degree to which this act of self-making could be shared—as if the self were no essential thing but an entity produced from the social interaction that language affords us. "I had fiddled with and fiddled with the lines, trying to join the two versions," says Bidart about one of Lowell's greatest poems, "Waking Early Sunday Morning." Lowell admitted that he did the same thing, ultimately failing to merge the two versions, and there is not just consolation but also a kind of euphoria in what he said next: "they both exist." To exist simultaneously as two selves, two persons, may have been Lowell's greatest wish. He was a poet who needed more than one person in order to write a poem, a poet who (more notoriously) often incorporated another person's language into his poems.

Two versions of "The Mills of the Kavanaughs," the long poem standing between the New Critical Lowell of *Lord Weary's Castle* (1946) and the confessional Lowell of *Life Studies* (1959), also exist. This poem is nobody's favorite (Randall Jarrell likened it to "a piece of music that consisted of nothing but climaxes"), but in the process of remaking it, Lowell forged the self on which all subsequent acts of self-making would depend. In the first version of the fourth stanza, published in the *Kenyon Review* early in 1951, Anne Kavanaugh thinks of her dead husband, who once attempted to strangle her: "She dreams he is Saint Patrick come to squire / Her home from school." In the version of the stanza published in "The Mills of the Kavanaughs" later in 1951, she turns not to Catholicism but to pagan mythology.

> She thinks of Daphne — Daphne could outrun
> The birds, and saw her swiftness tire the sun,
> And yet, perhaps, saw nothing to admire
> Beneath Apollo, when his crackling fire
> Stood rooted, half unwilling to undo
> Her laurel branches dropping from the blue.

The swerve from St. Patrick to Daphne, patron saint of metamorphosis, speaks of Lowell's own desire to change: as he wrote and rewrote the poem, Lowell was in the process of rejecting his adopted Catholicism, an act that would subsequently become associated with his rejection of meter and rhyme in the poems of *Life Studies*. Lowell did not alter the form of "The Mills of the Kavanaughs" (both versions are written in rhymed sixteen-line stanzas), but he drastically reduced the entire poem's investment in Catholicism, embracing a worldview in which change is the ultimate value. The revision consequently allows us to see that there is no natural relationship between the form and the ideology of the poem: a strict organicism (traditional thinking in traditional forms, free thinking in free forms) is in no way inevitable.

The most interesting poets who came of age in the immediate wake of modernism, Oppen and Lowell among them, wrote poems in which it is impossible to find consistently predictable associations between formal procedures and ideological underpinnings. That Lowell's poems have sometimes appeared to reinforce those associations is a testament to the ways in which his power as a maker of taste has occluded his power as a maker of poems. For without a strong sense of Lowell's struggle to remake himself in the years leading up to *Life Studies*, early readers were at liberty to perceive this book as a strategic rejection of what they took to be the late-modernist values of T. S. Eliot's New Critical acolytes, such as Allen Tate. As a result, the sound of *Life Studies* quickly became the sound of authenticity in American poetry — a poetry that seems to eschew high artifice, opening itself to speech, skirting the edge of prose. For the innumerable poets influenced by Lowell, such a poetry did indeed represent a rejection of artifice; but the Lowell of *Life Studies* was nothing but a maker — a poet who forged the apparently natural idiom on which other poets were to depend.

Listen to the final lines of "Terminal Days at Beverly Farms," a poem from *Life Studies* about the death of Lowell's father.

Each morning at eight-thirty,
inattentive and beaming,
loaded with his "calc" and "trig" books,
his clipper ship statistics,
and his ivory slide rule,
Father stole off with the *Chevie*
to loaf in the Maritime Museum at Salem.
He called the curator
"the commander of the Swiss Navy."

Father's death was abrupt and unprotesting.
His vision was still twenty-twenty.
After a morning of anxious, repetitive smiling,
his last words to Mother were:
"I feel awful."

Throughout these lines, the names of things (slide rule, Chevie, Maritime Museum) feel unalterable, and things themselves accumulate with little reason. Even if Lowell's father wishes for a world of imaginative possibility, his substitution of the words "commander of the Swiss Navy" for curator seems poignantly ineffectual. He feels merely "awful" because the language of his world will not allow him to change anything. This is the poet's greatest nightmare: Lowell's father is doomed to be no one other than himself.

Listen in contrast to Elizabeth Bishop's "The Bight," which ends with the words "awful but cheerful."

There is a fence of chicken wire along the dock
Where, glinting like little plowshares,
The blue-gray shark tails are hung up to dry
For the Chinese-restaurant trade.
Some of the little white boats are still piled up
against each other, or lie on their sides, stove in,
and not yet salvaged, if they ever will be, from the last bad storm,
like torn-open, unanswered letters.
The bight is littered with old correspondences.
Click. Click. Goes the dredge,
and brings up a dripping jawful of marl.
All the untidy activity continues,
awful but cheerful.

Bishop surveys the water at low tide. It is sheer but reveals nothing of interest; the dredge goes click, click. Yet the feeling evoked by this scene is not merely awful, because the poem's language is forever slipping into new connotations. Shark tails glint like plowshares, the little white boats are piled up like unanswered letters, and the bight is littered with old "correspondences": figuratively in the sense that only boats, not letters or plowshares, are present; literally in the sense that, as Baudelaire put it in the poem "Correspondences," our world is made up of nothing but figures — "forests of symbols" in which any given word brings to mind another word. The language of "The Bight" not only renders a vivid scene but encourages us to imagine the scene as different from itself. In contrast, Lowell's poem employs strategically flat diction in order to suppress the connotations on which a sense of imaginative possibility depends.

For years, Lowell's achievement overshadowed Bishop's, partly because the style Lowell forged in *Life Studies* became so extremely influential. But throughout *Life Studies*, Lowell's style is always in the service of sensibility: the diction of "Terminal Days" is almost comically precise in order to render a mind that fears imaginative possibility. As the notion of confessional poetry gained prominence, subsequent poets unhinged Lowell's style — the flattened rhythms, the avoidance of egregiously figurative language — from its rendering of a particular sensibility, transforming the style into an all-purpose way of denoting experience at large.

But even as this began to happen, Lowell had remade himself again: in the magazine version of "Waking Early Sunday Morning," he turned to rhymed tetrameter couplets, emphasizing the necessity of remaking a poetic idiom rather than relying on the readymade.

Time to grub up and junk the year's
output, a dead wood of dry verse:
dim confession, coy revelation,
liftings, listless self-imitation,
whole days when I could hardly speak,
came pluming home unshaven, weak
and willing to read anyone
things done before and better done.

This brilliant stanza sounds like Lowell, though it does not sound exactly like the Lowell of *Life Studies* or the Lowell of *The Mills of the Kavanaughs*. Both describing and embodying Lowell's need to change, the stanza was not included in the final version of "Waking Early Sunday Morning."

"Dim confession, coy revelation," said Lowell not of his imitators but of his imitations of himself. These were not words to which Lowell was often attracted, whatever their currency. "Because Robert Lowell is widely, perhaps indelibly associated with the term 'confessional,'" says Bidart, "it seems appropriate and even necessary to discuss how 'confessional' poetry is not confession." This needs to be said, but the saying makes Lowell feel like the victim of his own unwieldy power. Like only a handful of other poets (Eliot most vividly), Lowell had the great misfortune of having created the taste by which he was judged—first with approbation and, more recently, since the taste was strong enough to generate its opposite, with reproach. Meanwhile, some of the most compulsively well-made poems of the twentieth century remain overshadowed by the legend of the man who made them.

VII

Very Rich Hours

Frank Bidart's *In the Western Night: Collected Poems, 1965–1990*, concludes with a long poem called "The First Hour of the Night." A companion poem, "The Second Hour of the Night," appears at the end of the book *Desire*, published in 1997. That these poems are linked in the mind of their maker is clear, but the poems also stand comfortably alone. With the appearance of "The Third Hour of the Night," the concluding poem of Bidart's *Star Dust*, published eight years later, the first two poems are transformed.

After sex & metaphysics, —
. . . what?

What you have made.

Coming near the end of "The Third Hour of the Night," these lines ask us to read the three poems in sequence. Together, the poems offer a journey through discrete but overlapping aspects of the human psyche: metaphysics (or the burden of certainty) is the subject of the first hour, sex (or the terror of fulfilled desire) is the subject of the second, and the impulse to make (or the capacity for destruction) is the subject of the third. The three poems share certain structural and formal strategies, but there is no template, no synchronic formula: rather, the poems seduce us with the promise that coherence will simultaneously be revealed and unraveled over time. Power (or the acquisition of false mastery) is the subject of "The Fourth Hour of the Night," which appeared suddenly in 2017, twelve years after the third hour. Could there be a fifth, a sixth?

Behind the titles of these poems stands the Egyptian myth of the hours of the night. In the *Book of Gates*, the most complete version of which is found on the sarcophagus of Seti I, the sun must travel every night through the twelve divisions of the underworld before it is reborn at sunrise. Bidart makes no reference to this myth throughout the poems, but he does characterize it briefly in a little poem that precedes "The First Hour of the Night" in *In the Western Night*.

After the sun
Fell below the horizon of the west,

THE SUN-GOD

(according to words carved
on the sarcophagus of the pharaoh Seti I)

each night, during the twelve hours of the night, must
journey through
THE WORLD THAT IS BENEATH THE WORLD, —
. . . must

meet, once again, the dead.

The hour that must follow the eleventh hour

Is blank within my eye: —
I do not know what will make the sun rise again.

In itself, this myth is not crucial to our experience of the poem; as Pound said of the presence of the *Odyssey* within Joyce's *Ulysses*, the myth is essential to the making of the poem but not inevitably the reader's affair. What Bidart says *about* the myth, however, *is* crucial. First, his sense that the twelfth hour is unimaginable reminds us that "The Hours of the Night" is an unfinishable enterprise, a deliberately open-ended work of art whose shape will be determined by the vagaries of the life of its maker, not a myth. Second, Bidart's remark about the similarity of each hour points to the largest thematic contours of the sequence: in every hour, no matter what its particular concern (metaphysics, sex, making) we "must / meet, once again, the dead." At large, Bidart's journey through the landscape of the human psyche is driven by his unwavering sense of how we are made, even in the act of making, from forces outside ourselves, forces that can never be erased although they might be transformed.

Bidart is an immensely literary and a profoundly philosophical poet, but the poetry rarely seems learned or idea-driven. For while the language of the "Hours of the Night" embodies complicated notions of selfhood and identity, the poems dramatize these notions in a concatenation of narrative and lyric moments that is gripping to read.

*figures, postures from scenes that the eye cannot
entirely decipher, story haunting the eye with its*

resonance, unseen ground that explains nothing. . . .

These lines from "The Third Hour of the Night" describe Cellini's statue of Perseus holding up the severed head of the Medusa: adorning the base of the statue are several ancillary works by Cellini, smaller statues of Danaë, Jupiter, Mercury, and Minerva. The lines also characterize the structure of the "Hours of the Night," in which a central narrative event is similarly surrounded (sometimes overwhelmed) by briefer, more cryptic lyrics. In the first hour, the central event is a long dream inspired by Volpato's etching of Raphael's *School of Athens*; the dreamer is not named but is associated with the philosopher Wilhelm Dilthey, father of modern hermeneutics. In the second hour, the central event is the story of Myrrha, narrated in the third person. And in the third hour, the central event is a long monologue by Cellini himself, culminating in an account of the creation of the Perseus. The fourth hour is centered around the life of a boy named Temujin, who grows up to become Genghis Khan, founder of the Mongol empire.

Each of these central narratives stands in a particular relation to its poem's ancillary pieces. Because the whole of "The First Hour of the Night" is narrated by Dilthey (or someone like him), the pieces seem more plainly interrelated, connected by the ligaments of a single psyche. But in the second hour, which doesn't encourage us to imagine a consistent speaker, the ancillary pieces seem more obliquely related. The pieces become even more distinct in the third hour, in which radically different speakers beg to be merged: here, the relationships between the pieces seem more provocatively mysterious than the relationships between the poems at large. While some modes of coherence fade, however, others glow more brightly: what once seemed like relatively unimportant moments in the first hour now seem crucial because of their relationship to the central narrative of the third or fourth hour. Something of the grandeur of the encyclopedic masterworks of modernism hangs over the sequence at large, and, as is the case with *Ulysses*, the basic framework is easily dispatched with while the real pleasure lies in the indigestible detail.

Consider the most crucial passage from "The First Hour of the Night." Early in the poem, the narrator has told the son of a deceased friend about a pony he loved as a child: looking into the pony's face, he felt himself to be mirrored utterly, his identity consolidated. Later, when the narrator falls asleep beneath Volpato's etching of Plato and Aristotle surrounded by fellow philosophers, he dreams that the once coherent-seeming traditions of Western philosophy collapse into a discord so immense that it challenges the very project of human thought. Then, when the face of his dead friend appears to him, the face becomes a cloud,

and, as if he were looking in a mirror, the dreamer feels his own
identity disintegrate.

    as if the soul, delivered over unconscious and

defenseless not only to this world of
things, but to its own DARKNESS, —

. . . flinging itself into the compensations that the world
and its own self

offer it, but finding the light of *self-knowledge*
only through
                mediation, through WORKS and SIGNS, —

. . . seeing and remaking itself within that broken
mirror made by all the things that it has
inherited and remade, —

. . . in the end, alienates its being in them.

Here, rather than being solidified by the act of reflection, the
human soul discovers itself dispersed by the very forces that
have made it, by the very things it has made. Initially horrifying, this moment is ultimately the source of immense consolation: the dreamer is liberated from the certainty he thought he
enjoyed when looking into the face of the pony—the same certainty he came to associate with the logical progression of Western thought. The price of certainty, the poem suggests, is the
inability ever to change, and the first hour concludes with the
dreamer's exhausted realization that he is free to transform his
inheritance, rather than attempting pointlessly to erase it. This
will become the wrenching theme of "The Second Hour of the
Night," in which Myrrha, desperately in love with her own father,

begs to be transformed, to "lose her body to an alien / body not chosen."

Now consider a passage in "The First Hour of the Night" that, until the publication of the third hour, seemed relatively insignificant, perhaps even ornamental. With the collapse of the temple in which Plato and Aristotle stand, says the dreamer,

the frozen facial mask of
Medusa, hung on Athena's shield, suddenly

smiled. *Smirked.*

The Medusa, destroyed when Perseus holds a mirror to her face, is obviously central to "The Third Hour of the Night," but it's now clear that her presence hovers over all the poems: to see oneself reflected in something other than oneself is simultaneously to be constituted and disintegrated, conceived and killed. "Making is the mirror in which we see ourselves," says Bidart in one of the shorter poems in *Star Dust*, but the project of both the third and fourth "Hours of the Night" is to rid this statement of any residual sentimentality. For while we may recognize that we are made by forces outside ourselves, and while we may recognize that those inerasable forces might be transformed, we must still recognize the terror of transformation. To see ourselves in what we make, Bidart suggests, is to confront our mortality, and this happens in the poems, as it happens in life, over time. There is no other way to live.

Bidart himself was made in Bakersfield, California—"a culture," he would remember, "that was intolerable to me." In 1957, he fled first to the University of California at Riverside, where he discovered the poems of Eliot and Pound, and then to Harvard, where he discovered the poets Robert Lowell and Elizabeth Bishop, who became to him something more than mentors or friends: "I had been given, miraculously," Bidart remembers, "the chance to be the 'good son' rather than the 'bad son.'"

From Bishop, the good son inherited an almost maniacal passion for accuracy; from Lowell, an appetite for emotional extremity so intense that it threatened to make extremity feel like the norm.

I have LEARNED

my NATURE . . .

I am insane,—
. . . or evil.

Such typographical effects, at once meticulous and unhinged, distinguish all of Bidart's early poems, beginning with "Herbert White," a monologue spoken by a necrophiliac, and culminating in "The War of Vaslav Nijinksy," from which I've just quoted. But by the time Bidart wrote "The Second Hour of the Night," most of these effects had fallen away. Even more interestingly, when Bidart collected "The First Hour of the Night" in *Half-Life*, his 2017 collected poems, he rewrote the poem, not altering much of its language but drastically reducing its use of idiosyncratic punctuation, italicization, and capitalization. This passage from the earlier version—

—What one thinker confidently
ASSERTED,
                another *spurned* as ILLUSION

—became this:

—What one thinker confidently
asserted, another spurned as illusion

Given the unfolding project of the poems, the way they clarify themselves over time, why did this transformation need to happen?

A crucial passage from "The Second Hour of the Night" re-tells Ovid's telling of the story of Myrrha, who was possessed by the desire to sleep with her father, Cinyras, the king of Cypress.

As Myrrha is drawn down the dark corridor toward her father

not free not to desire

what draws her forward is neither COMPULSION nor FREE
WILL: —

or at least freedom, here *choice*, is not to be
imagined as action upon

preference: no creature is free to choose what
allows it its most powerful, and most secret, release:

I fulfill it, because I contain it —
it prevails, because it is within me —

it is a heavy burden, setting up longing to enter that
realm to which I am called from within . . .

As Myrrha is drawn down the dark corridor toward her father

not free not to choose

she thinks, *To each soul its hour.*

Myrrha is not the agent of her own desire. What she desires is her fate, which is inside her in the sense that it is essentially hers, outside her in the sense that it is other than her: the self is deter-mined by forces that will eventually destroy the integrity of the self. Moreover, while these lines describe this terrifying economy of selfhood, they also embody it: the lines "no creature is free to choose what / allows it its most powerful, and most secret, re-lease" are not original to Frank Bidart; he has lifted this phrase from T. S. Eliot's introduction to the selected poems of Mari-anne Moore, lineating Eliot's prose: "We all have to choose what-ever subject-matter allows us the most personal and most secret release."

The implication here is that Bidart has had no choice but to appropriate Eliot's language, in the same way that Myrrha has had no choice but to walk down the corridor to her father's bed: like the human self, linguistic utterance is radically overdeter-mined by forces outside the utterer. *"We fill pre-existing forms,"* says Bidart apropos of Myrrha's fate, *"and when / we fill them, change them and are changed."* Here, Bidart is appropriating his own language, lineating a sentence that he has used elsewhere to describe aesthetic rather than erotic fate: "We fill pre-existing forms and when we fill them we change them and are changed."

Lengthy passages from each of the hours have been carved from the prose of Wilhelm Dilthey, Hector Berlioz, and Benve-nuto Cellini; Bidart has always been a poet who embraces other lives, other voices, beginning with the monologue "Herbert White." But in the early poems, Bidart's idiosyncratic typography and punctuation strain as if to embody an independent voice, one that exists apart from the language of the poem, and the allure of the poetry lies in this straining to transcend itself. In the "Hours of the Night," in contrast, the voices feel compromised and yet paradoxically more present, woven from a tissue of competing linguistic strands. Gone is the straining, along with much of the idiosyncratic typography and punctuation required to enact it: in its place we feel the rapt inhabitation of the process through which a voice might be posited, rising from the page rather than straining to transcend it. Like the soul of Myrrha, the "Hours of the Night" are forged from forces of which they are not in charge. To be is to have been derived, to speak is to have been spoken.

"The purpose of playing," says Hamlet to the troupe of actors in his play, is "to hold, as 'twere, the mirror up to nature." This passage has haunted Bidart all his life; in "Borges and I" he remembers lying on his bed as a child, listening to a recording of Lawrence Olivier reciting the speech. But inasmuch as Bidart has absorbed its wisdom about the purpose of art, he does not just make poems that are, in the Aristotelian sense, imitations of an action; his poems are themselves actions, and, finally, the most crucial act of mirroring is the one that takes place between the "Hours of the Night" and their readers.

O you who looking within the mirror discover in
gratitude how common, how lawful your desire,

before the mirror
anoint your body with myrrh

precious　　　　bitter resin

Self-knowledge doesn't save Myrrha from her fate; she understands everything. She can be delivered from herself only by becoming something inhuman—a tree, whose tears are myrrh, a gift fit for the birth and the death of prophets. When we finish reading her story, we too know everything; insight is ours. But unlike Myrrha, we have been transformed. More precisely, we have lived through the verbal contraption of the poem and come to recognize ourselves in aspects of human experience that initially seemed alien to us—exaggerated, grotesque, bizarre. By reading Bidart, we discover the Medusa within.

VIII

Potential Space

"I have crossed out passages. / I have severely trimmed and cleared," says Jorie Graham in the opening poem of *Swarm*, her seventh collection of poems. Each of the books preceding it — *Region of Unlikeness, Materialism, The Errancy* — was more expansive than the one before, Graham's run-on sentences becoming ever longer, her syntax ever more breathlessly incomplete. But in *Swarm* the poems feel suddenly chastened, unseduced by the allure of something more to say. Lyric poems typically take place in identifiable locations, some of them historical verifiable, but the location of the stripped-down poems of *Swarm* not only feels troubled; the poems also give us only a little trouble to go on. They're happening now, but where?

What are you thinking?
Here on the bottom?
What do you squint clear for yourself
up there through the surface?

Explain   door ajar.
Explain   hopeth all.
Explain   surface   future   subject-of.

Pierce.

Be swift.

(Let's wade again.)

(Offstage: pointing-at)
(Offstage: stones placing themselves on eyes)

Here: tangle and seaweed

current   diagram   how deep?   I have

forgotten.

Don't leave me. I won't.

As these opening lines of "For One Must Want / To Shut the Other's Gaze" insist, they are located *here*: on the bottom of the ocean, beneath the surface, among tangle and seaweed. But however adamantly imagined, that location doesn't help us much to read the poem; like most of the poems of *Swarm*, it feels incomplete—as if we were challenged to imagine the interior space below the surface without any knowledge of the surface.

The ocean to which the poem gestures is more obviously metaphorical than literal: "So we must meet apart— / You there—I—here— / With just the Door ajar / That Oceans are," says Emily Dickinson in a poem that Graham's title misquotes. As for Dickinson, the ocean is for Graham a space of unbearable separation that paradoxically preserves the possibility of union, a place where the meeting of selves creates not understanding but a craving for explanation. And while the poem honors that craving, it also refuses to satisfy it: while insisting that "the real plot was invisible," it also asks us to "name the place." As if to stress that we've come to this poem not for knowledge but for the experience of what it feels like to know something, "For One Must Want / To Shut the Other's Gaze" concludes with the question with which it began: "What are you thinking?"

Following this question is the title poem of *Swarm*. Its subtitle answers the injunction to name the place (*"Todi, 1996"*), and its first five lines offer a narrative perspicuity that is stripped away throughout the rest of the volume.

I wanted you to listen to the bells,
holding the phone out the one small window
to where I thought
the ringing was —

Vespers scavenging the evening air,
headset fisted against the huge dissolving

where I stare at the tiny holes in the receiver's transatlantic
opening
to see evening-light and then churchbells

send their regrets, slithering in —
in there a white flame charged with duplication —.
I had you try to listen, bending down into the mouthpiece to
whisper, hard,

can you hear them (two petals fall and then the   is wholly
changed) (yes) (and then another yes like a vertebrate
enchaining)

yes yes yes yes

We were somebody.

In these lines, "the long ocean between us" is no figure but the Atlantic Ocean; the speaker in Italy telephones the auditor in the United States, beckoning him to listen to the church bells. If "For One Must Want / To Shut the Other's Gaze" is about an intimacy that depends on the preservation of distinctions, "The

Swarm" is about the desperately misguided attempt to overcome those distinctions, wearing away the edges on which the passion of intimacy (for both the lover and the reader) depends.

For while the poem begins matter-of-factly, its expositional manner seeming to capitulate to the injunction to "name the place," the poem quickly reveals the complexity of even the simplest act of naming. We cannot rest comfortably with our knowledge of the literal because language is inevitably threatening to transform the literal into the figurative. For what are the bells "scavenging" the evening air? Why does the speaker "stare at" the receiver rather than listening to it? Is the speaker really asking the auditor to hear "two petals fall," or are the petals an emblem of the difficulty of hearing the bells from across the ocean? In any case, this increasingly desperate attempt to name the place and surmount the distance collapses in the simple declaration that "we were somebody." The implication is that the relationship between the speaker and the auditor is itself a figure for the relationship between the poem and its reader: to name the location flatly, to leave nothing unexplained, is to render the poem undesirable and the reader unacquainted with desire. As "Underneath (1)," the poem following "The Swarm," puts it,

> you were too
> close for me to make
> out in-
>
> dividual words.

Our craving for a more perfect union may be inevitable, but to satisfy the craving is to be denied the expectation that something (we don't yet know what) could be left to discover.

That expectation is crucial to our experience of any poem because it is an inevitable part of our experience of figurative language. Graham's language feels less determinedly referential than Bishop's or Lowell's, but her poem is not written in a different language; we are not at liberty to decide when words will have meanings. We may be more or less aware of the intricate relationship of figures to things, however, and in this sense "For One Must Want / To Shut the Other's Gaze" foregrounds the complexity of any poem's relationship to its place. All poems are troubled about their own locations because their language is troubled by its referentiality; they recognize that the effort to include a clear sense of a location in the poem may become indistinguishable from the effort to omit it.

Why did Graham need to foreground this trouble so vigorously in the poems of *Swarm*? The greatest danger for Graham has always been a breathless rhetoric of desperation, a way of inhabiting language that makes almost any human experience — picking up a stick, delivering a child's leotard — feel inflated to apocalyptic proportions. As her poems accumulated, however powerfully, they threatened to make every moment of human experience feel unrelievedly dire, flattening experience by eradicating the possibility of the truly exceptional moment.

Neither is this danger unfamiliar, as the trajectory of Bidart's career suggests. Whether extending the popularized notion of Lowell's confessionalism or turning against it, the modern American lyric has tended to associate authenticity with extremity, and throughout *Swarm* Graham checks this tendency by cutting her more typically extravagant syntax down to the smallest possible units: along with syntax, a strong sense of place, voice, and story also fall away, producing lyrics that, when they first appeared, seemed to many readers bewilderingly parched. But in retrospect, these poems seem to me Graham's crucial achievement. And since the publication of *Swarm* in 2000, Graham's challenge has been to return to the extravagance of syntax, of story, without raising her voice.

"How can I believe in that," asked John Keats when he first saw the Lake District he had come to know from Wordsworth's poems. He was not referring to the sublime grandeur of the landscape, the mountains and waterfalls: "What astonishes me more than any thing is the tone, the coloring, the slate, the stone, the moss, the rock-weed." Keats's question is the epigraph to Graham's *Never*, published in 2002, and the poems embody a dramatically patient attempt simply to record the tone of things as they appear in particular locations at particular times. "Over a dock railing, I watch the minnows," begins the first poem in the book. "I am beneath the tree," begins the second.

But even as one makes the decision to record the object world as faithfully as possible, locating the object in space and time, how does one evade the temporality of the act of recording? Even if language were fully capable of locking the object in a particular moment in time, would one *want* to do so? Graham begins "Afterwards" by recording her observation of two starlings emerging from a hawthorn, their bodies literalizing the presence of their song, her syntax recovering the extravagance she had denied herself in *Swarm*.

> When two
> appear in flight, straight to the child-sized pond of
> melted snow,
> and thrash, dunk, rise, shake, rethrashing, reconfiguring through
> reshufflings and resettlings the whole body of integrated
> featherwork,
> they shatter open the blue-and-tree-tip filled-up gaze of
> the lawn's two pools,
> breaking and ruffling all the crisp true sky we had seen living
> down in that tasseled
> earth. How shall we say this *happened*?

Graham emphasizes the ambiguity of the word "happened" here, but the word "this" is equally difficult to calibrate. Is "this" the flight of the starlings, their shattering of the pool of melted snow? If so, why does this "child-sized pond" become "two pools" after the starlings have entered it? Is "this" the fracturing of the pool itself? And is this fracturing an event that actually happens or a metaphor for what appears to have happened, the "breaking" of the "true sky" reflected in the water? Throughout *Never*, Graham is poised "head-down and over some one / thing," but her quiet devotion to her place becomes more vexed to the degree that it becomes more passionate.

Of course, Graham thrives on vexation; it is the record of her being in the world. But inasmuch as Graham is poised, head-down over waves or seagulls or starlings, she wants us to feel that her words inevitably distract us from what they also point toward: the more pressure Graham places on a word's denotative power, the more manifold its proliferating associations become. In addition, since the starling or the seagull or the wave is constantly in motion, the precisely denotative word is always lagging behind or lurching ahead of the object. In the final movement of "Gulls," which begins with seagulls that act like poets, head bent down "over some one / thing," the poet's language is likened to a seagull, moving swiftly over the sand.

> my clutch of
>   words
> swaying and stemming from my
>   saying, no
> echo. No stopping on the temporarily exposed and drying rock
>   out there
> to rub or rest where nothing else
>   grows.
> And truly swift over the sands.
> As if most afraid of being re-
>   peated.
> Preferring to be dissolved to
>   designation,
> backglancing stirrings,
> wedged-in between unsaying and
>   forgetting—
> what an enterprise—spoken out by

me as if
to *still* some last place, place becoming even as I speak
unspeakable—

There is no crisis of representation here, no crisis of selfhood. To recognize that place becomes increasingly unspeakable as it is spoken is simply to recognize that we inhabit the world intimately—not in spite of language but because of it. So if locations are obscured in the chastened poems of *Swarm*, how should they be said to have been emphasized in *Never*? Readers who found *Swarm* excessively difficult found *Never* more immediately apprehendable, but what matters about these two books is not their difference from each other; what matters is the way in which their difference from each other forces us to inhabit the question of their similarity. One book cannot help but to conjure locations as it disperses them; the other cannot help but to disperse the locations it conjures.

Which is a way of saying, once again, that poems are works of art that people make out of words. In "a creative and spontaneous being," says D. W. Winnicott, one finds "a capacity for the use of symbols," by which he means language in general. Children spend most of their time in a psychic space that is neither completely internal nor completely external—the "potential space" of play. But adults may too readily capitulate either to a world of inanimate objects, on the one hand, or to a world of uncontested fantasy, on the other: the healthy adult continues to live in increasingly complex and tenuous versions of potential space.

Focusing our attention on how language slips between the literal and the figurative, the imagined and the real, poetry creates that space. All language has this capacity. But because we don't necessarily expect a poem to be useful in obvious or immediate ways, the language of poetry is liberated to create that space aggressively: call it the beach at Jorie's house, it is the place where we live.

IX

Moving On

A girl grows up in a working-class family in New Jersey, the eldest of four children. Her mother is a waitress, her father works nights. The girl collects things, pebbles, marbles, charms—things that speak to her because of where she found them. She reads a lot of books. In the Philadelphia bus depot, she finds a book called *Illuminations*, which she pockets because she's attracted to the author's face. Why was a copy of Arthur Rimbaud's *Illuminations* waiting for her at the bus depot?

In 1967, when she drops out of college and moves to Brooklyn, she meets a beautiful boy. Like her, he feels destined to be an artist. But while she draws a little, writes a little, occasionally sings, the boy is focused, convinced that their artistic yearnings are not childish dreams. The boy grows up to be the photographer Robert Mapplethorpe; the girl will be named a Commandeur des Arts et des Lettres by the French Ministry of Culture. She keeps a lock of his hair, a goatskin tambourine, a vial of his ashes.

Over the past four decades, Patti Smith has expressed herself as a musician, a painter, a photographer, an actress, an activist, a poet, a memoirist. She has recorded eleven albums, beginning with the groundbreaking *Horses*, released in 1975, which featured Mapplethorpe's now-iconic photograph of Smith on the cover, black jacket tossed over her shoulder, Sinatra-style. Her photographs and paintings have been exhibited in the Museum of Modern Art in New York and in the Pompidou Center in Paris.

The first of her nine (depending on what you count) books of poems, *Seventh Heaven*, appeared in 1972, the first of her three memoirs, *Woolgathering*, in 1992. Her second memoir, *Just Kids*, an account of her relationship with Mapplethorpe, won the National Book Award in 2010, and her third, *M Train*, which she calls a book about nothing, appeared in 2015.

A recording artist is inevitably going to be more famous than a poet of immense success, and while Patti Smith is known best as a musician, writing has always lain at the center of her achievement; her drawings are often made of words, long strings of miniscule, almost indecipherable script, and her song lyrics often aspire to the combination of visceral directness and oracular mystery that one associates with great poems from Rimbaud to Ashbery: "On a golden road / night is a mongrel / believe or explode." But it's one thing to write a great rock-n-roll lyric and another thing to sustain a book like *M Train*, her most charismatic writerly performance. The line "wop bop a loo lop a lop bam boom," from Little Richard's "Tutti Frutti," is a thrilling line in a song, but how would you describe it as great writing? Bob Dylan may be the recipient of the Nobel Prize in literature, but we don't necessarily expect his often wildly disjunctive lyrics ("Walk on your tip toes / Don't tie no bows / Better stay away from those / That carry round a fire hose") to hold our attention on the page as rivetingly as they do when we hear them sung.

How then *does* a poem hold our attention on the page? These lines from "When the Sun Went Down" appear in *A Wave*, the 1984 volume of poems in which John Ashbery's mature style was most perfectly achieved, consolidating the advances of *Three Poems* and *Self-Portrait in a Convex Mirror*.

There are times when music steals a march on us,
Is suddenly perplexingly nearer, flowing in my wrist;
Is the true and dirty words you whisper nightly
As the book closes like a collapsing sheet, a blur
Of all kinds of connotations ripped from the hour and tossed

Like jewels down a well; the answer, also,
To the question that was on my mind but that I've forgotten,
Except in the way certain things, certain nights, come together.

Ashbery's mature style depends on the swift juxtaposition of different levels of diction; the endlessly inventive leaping between
these levels—*music, wrist, dirty words, book, sheet, jewels, well*—
constitutes the pleasure of the poetry, the language just slightly
outpacing our capacity to take it in. One feels this pleasure also
in a Dylan song, but in an Ashbery poem the energy of the diction is at every second in tension with a contrary impulse—one
that doesn't necessarily need to be active in an effective song, in
which the language has the music to fall back on: however wildly
disjunctive his diction, Ashbery's syntax is as meticulous as Dr.
Johnson's.

The first line of the sentence I've quoted from "When the Sun
Went Down" is hypotactic: that is, it contains two clauses (*there
are times* and *music steals a march*), the second dependent on the
first.

There are times when music steals a march

The following seven lines offer three parallel variations on the
dependent clause, all of them linked to the initial independent
clause (*when music is suddenly perplexingly nearer; when music is
the true and dirty words; when music is the answer to the question*).
We're made to wait a long time for the third variation, for it is delayed by four additional dependent clauses attached to the second (*that you whisper; as the book closes; that are ripped; that are
tossed*). And finally, as the sentence concludes, the third variation
is itself extended by three more dependent clauses (*that was on
my mind; that I've forgotten; except in the way things come together*).

But the power of Ashbery's poem is due not simply to the fact
that his syntax is grammatically impeccable: because we generally associate the hypotactic syntax he favors with the construc-

tion of causes and effects of arguments or in arguments (the multiple clauses linked by subordinating conjunctions like *because,
that, when,* or *since*), Ashbery's sentences sound as if they make
rational sense, even when his diction feels chaotic, the semantic
links between multiple clauses obscure. A song lyric that courts
chaos depends similarly on the often simply repetitive structure
of the music, which is why otherwise brilliant lyrics by Dylan or
Smith, so seductive in the ear, may fall flat on the page. This is
also why so many of Ashbery's imitators, who mimic the freedom of his diction but not the rigor of his syntax, also fall flat. In
order to write for the page as she does in *M Train*, Patti Smith had
to fall in love with syntax.

She looks around a room. What does she see?

> Things beyond socks or glasses: Kevin Shields's EBow, a snap-
> shot of a sleepy-faced Fred, a Burmese offering bowl, Margot
> Fonteyn's ballet slippers, a misshapen clay giraffe formed by
> my daughter's hands. I pause before my father's chair.

Reading these sentences, we feel Smith pause at the chair because her syntax shifts: the first person enters, followed by the
first active verb—*I pause.* Prior to this moment, things have
followed one another as if of their own accord. Now the mind
enters the proceedings, but the syntax returns to the same kind
of listlike accumulation of things.

> My father sat at his desk, in this chair, for decades, writing
> checks, filling out tax forms, and working fervently on his
> own system for handicapping horses. Bundles of *The Morning
> Telegraph* were stacked against the wall. A journal wrapped in
> jeweler's cloth, noting wins and losses from imaginary bets,
> kept in the left-hand drawer.

Parallel phrases tumble on top of each other (*writing checks, fill-
ing out forms, working fervently*); then active verbs fall away again,

allowing noun phrases to nestle side by side as if they were themselves the things she is no longer observing in the room around
her but remembering from the past ("Bundles of *The Morning
Telegraph*" — "A journal wrapped in jeweler's cloth").

Then the mind returns: "When he died I inherited his desk
and chair." But not for long.

> Inside the desk was a cigar box containing canceled checks,
> nail clippers, a broken Timex watch, and a yellowed news-
> paper cutting of my beaming self in 1959, being awarded third
> prize in a national safety-poster contest.

This is how the life of Patti Smith enters the world of *M Train*,
which is always on the move: not as narrated event (*in 1959 I
was awarded third prize*) but as the by-product of her animating
dialogue with the things that bear the lives of people she loves,
people she's lost: her parents, her brother, her husband; Jean
Genet, Sylvia Plath, Enid Meadowcroft (author of *The Story of
Davy Crockett*). The conversation is at turns poignant, whimsical,
stern, but it is always deeply respectful of the otherness of things,
and, as a result, it is seductively dry-eyed especially at its moments of greatest emotional intensity: "You should sit on me,"
says her father's chair to her, but Smith can't bring herself to do
so: "We were never allowed to sit at my father's desk, so I don't
use his chair, just keep it near."

How precisely did Patti Smith become the writer of these
sentences? Throughout the later 1970s, Smith often opened her
concerts by reciting a prose-poem called "babelogue"; her album
Easter, released in 1978, features a recording of her reciting the
poem over Lenny Kaye's guitar, and the poem also appears in
Babel, a book published in the same year.

> i haven't fucked w/ the past but i've fucked plenty w/ the
> future. over the silk of skin are scars from the splinters of
> stages and walls i've caressed. each bolt of wood, like the log

of helen, was my pleasure. i would measure the success of a
night by the amount of piss and seed i could exude over the
columns that nestled the P/A. some nights i'd surprise every-
body by snapping on a skirt of green net sewed over w/ flat
metallic circles which dangled and flashed the lights were vio-
let and white.

These sentences are designed more to be performed than read,
and like a lot of people, I can attest to the fact that listening to
Smith recite this poem is completely thrilling; but over the decades, as Smith's sentences have moved from performance to
page, I've been more moved by the way she's become scrupulously attentive to the demands context makes on the act of
writing. Most rock-n-roll singers who write books do not write
crafted sentences, even though they've written brilliant song
lyrics; most visual artists do not write books at all. The opening
line of the Rolling Stones' "Honky Tonk Woman" ("I met a gin-
soaked bar-room queen in Memphis") is an iambic pentameter
line, one whose rhythm Shakespeare might have coveted, but nobody would expect Mick Jagger and Keith Richards to be inter-
ested in writing ten such lines in a row; nor would we fault them
for failing to do so.

You can witness Smith in the act of becoming the syntax-
driven writer she is today in her first memoir, *Woolgathering*. At
first, its sentences sound more like *Babel* than like *M Train*, more
like sentences to be performed.

> The cruel intensity of this process can produce a thing of
> beauty but oftentimes just a tear in the shimmering from
> which to wrest and wriggle. A spine of rope sliding an arena
> more remote and dazzling than ever.

But as you turn the pages of *Woolgathering*, you can feel the sentences change to the degree that Smith attempts not to embody

her thinking in a verbal stream of consciousness but to describe a sequence of things that provoke her thinking: the performance shifts to the action happening on the page. This is an account of the last day she spent with a beloved dog named Bambi.

It was in my mind to take her to all the places we loved. We would take one last walk to Red Clay Mountain and stop awhile by Rainbow Creek. I had a peanut butter sandwich wrapped in wax paper and some dog biscuits. I sat with Bambi at my feet and surveyed my domain. She would not eat her treats. She knows, I thought.

Here, Smith hasn't yet figured out how to make her syntax itself embody the accumulation of telltale things, as she does so effortlessly in *M Train*, but that impulse is nonetheless driving the prose: peanut butter sandwich, Rainbow Creek, Red Clay Mountain. The author of *M Train* wouldn't need to say, "It was in my mind to take her to all the places we loved," but you would understand this palpably to be the case.

Unlike *Woolgathering*, *M Train* is written from a perspective that feels posthumous. After the release of the album *Wave* in 1979, Smith moved to Detroit with her new husband, Fred Sonic Smith (the guitarist from the MC5). For a decade, they raised two children, they refurbished a boat; there was a scraggly pear tree in the yard. Then Mapplethorpe died of AIDS in 1989. Fred Smith died unexpectedly of a heart attack five years later, Smith's brother of a stroke just a month after that, and in 1996 Smith moved back to New York. She began recording and exhibiting regularly again; it was a productive, grief-fueled time.

"Now I have no trees," says Smith of her present self in *M Train*, "there is no crib or clothesline." At moments like this, she sounds like most any devoted parent in late middle age. And much of *M Train* is given over to accounts of the little rituals in the daily life of a woman living alone in the Village; if she finds someone sitting at her favorite table in her favorite café, a café whose closing she mourns throughout the whole book, she waits in the bathroom until the interloper leaves.

She also waits for something to come her way, and because Smith is not just any woman living in the Village, things come: an invitation to address a meeting of the Continental Drift Club in Berlin, an invitation to speak at the home of Frida Kahlo. But in Berlin she is ridiculed ("This isn't science, it's poetry!"), and in Mexico she falls violently ill. Travel, as the title of *M Train* suggests, is what Smith lives for, but *M* stands for *mental*: mental travel, mental train.

She drinks a cup of coffee. She remembers her mother brewing coffee in a percolator, waiting by the stove in her blue-flowered housecoat. In Detroit, because there were no nearby cafés, Smith brewed coffee too. But on Saturday mornings she would walk to the local 7/11 for a large black coffee and a glazed donut. Then she would sit behind a little whitewashed bait-and-tackle shop.

> To me it looked like Tangiers, though I had never been there. I sat on the ground in the corner surrounded by low white walls, shelving real time, free to rove the smooth bridge connecting past and present. My Morocco. I followed whatever train I wanted. I wrote without writing — of genies and hustlers and mythic travelers, my *vagabondia*. Then I would walk back home, happily satisfied, and resume my daily tasks. Even now, having at last been to Tangiers, my spot behind the bait store seems the true Morocco in my memory.

Coffee, her mother, Michigan, Morocco: Smith cherishes the dependably stable space she's crafted for herself in the Village, but her mind is always on the move. "By the time I got back to New York I had forgotten why I'd left," she says of the trip to Berlin, and the mental itineraries of *M Train* feel similarly linear, one thing leading inevitably to another thing, each one lovingly fondled, catalogued, preserved. Then it's time to feed the cats, time to brew the coffee.

Some things, however, are too painful. She opens her desk. She removes a small metal box: three fishing lures, one made of purple transparent rubber, like a Juicy Fruit. "Hello, Curly," she says to the lure, speaking to the object that speaks to her, remembering how she and Fred would go fishing on Lake Ann in Northern Michigan, how Fred taught her to cast, how he gave her "a portable Shakespeare rod whose parts fit like arrows in a carrying case shaped like a quiver." The satisfaction Smith takes in describing the rod, word by word, feels like the satisfaction she took in putting it together, taking it apart. "We want things we cannot have," she laments, and out tumble more things.

> I want to hear my mother's voice. I want to see my children as children. Hands small, feet swift. Everything changes. Boy grown, father dead, daughter taller than me, weeping from a bad dream. Please stay forever, I say to the things I know. Don't go. Don't grow.

Once again, the power of this passage is due not to the wisdom as such but to its nearly verbless accumulation of things, the rhythm progressing from punchy pairs of monosyllabic words ("Hands small, feet swift") to the slight lilt of words containing unstressed syllables ("Everything changes") to the amplitude of a completed clause ("Please stay forever, I say to the things I know"), before returning to the punchy two-beat rhythm with which it began: "Don't go. Don't grow." This writing is moving because, like all writing we want to read more than once, it moves.

"You, being a poet, know that all these awards and accolades do not diminish the suffering, the sacrifice, the blood, the sweat that all true poets have to go through," said Smith at a ceremony honoring John Ashbery as the recipient of the National Art Club's Medal of Honor. Smith is speaking here the language of the outlaw poet, a language she speaks more fluently than Ashbery. But like Rimbaud, the precursor she shares with Ashbery, Smith knows that a poet suffers to make sentences. This is why she so adamantly refers to *M Train* — a book fueled by the loss of her parents, the death of her husband, the grief of her children — as a book about nothing. The work is turning nothing into something, words on the page.

X

Disliking It

"What I should like to write," said Gustav Flaubert, toiling away at *Madame Bovary*, "is a book about nothing, a book dependent on nothing external, which would be held together by the internal strength of its style, just as the earth, suspended in the void, depends on nothing external for its support; a book which would have almost no subject, or at least in which the subject would be almost invisible."

Flaubert aspired to the condition of the high lyric poet, the presumption of the poet's isolation, the presumption (even more liberating to him) of the poet's irrelevance. If Galileo had said in verse that the earth travels around the sun, ventured Thomas Hardy, who at the end of the nineteenth century abandoned novels for poems, the Inquisition would have left him alone. Poets, especially American poets, are pretty much left alone, and sometimes this makes them petulant. Who wouldn't want to be as worldly, as relevant, as the novelists Hardy or Flaubert, who themselves coveted the freedom of a poet's obscurity? Many American poets writing in the twenty-first century assume that poets should be what Pound called *acknowledged* legislators. Is that ambition inevitably a good thing?

"There was a bird, once," says Carl Phillips in "Against His Quitting the Torn Field," a poem from *Pastoral*, his fourth collection of poems and, in retrospect, the collection that established the voice we recognize as his alone. *There was a bird, once*. Then, in a gesture typical of his wavering, self-questioning poems, Phillips corrects himself.

Or, shorn of bird — call only —
a calling-to that seemed
it would never end, be done
raveling.

Phillips's poems are themselves *call only*. They ravel down the page. They conjure a world in which experience and the loss of experience are nearly impossible to distinguish from each other. As the great classicist Bruno Snell said of Virgil in *The Discovery of the Mind*, Carl Phillips "has ceased to see anything but what is important to him: tenderness and warmth and delicacy of feeling." But while I quote this remark as praise, Snell intended it to be a condemnation not only of Virgil's *Eclogues* but of pastoral poetry in general — its artificiality, its otherworldliness, its lack of "any desire to do something about the suffering world."

The pastoral poem is to the lyric as cognac is to the wine from which it is twice distilled. Invented by Theocritus in the third century BCE, powerfully imitated by Virgil several centuries later, the pastoral is a poem about poetry, a lyric about lyricism: impossibly literary shepherds and goatherds lounge about an arcadian landscape, singing songs about love. Since Virgil, many of the pastoral's most egregiously artificial trappings have fallen away; there are no shepherds to be found in Phillips's poems. But the pastoral impulse — its delight in artifice, its delicacy of feeling, its disregard for the distractions of worldliness — remains alive and well, as does a long-standing disdain for such impulses. For the scholar Annabel Patterson, pastoral emphasizes the lyric poet's "exclusiveness, his difference from the civic 'we.'" When the poet Nuar Alsadir sees the words "Fuck Lyric" scrawled on the wall of a New York subway station, she resorts to prose. Claudia Rankine's *Citizen*, which describes itself as an "American Lyric," is made of fleeting observations and incomplete arguments, all in prose. Why would anyone advertise his poetry as pastoral? How is a poetry as elegantly disembodied as Phillips's to be received in such a climate of opinion?

At the conclusion of Virgil's first eclogue, the shepherd Meliboeus has been sent into exile, his lands confiscated in the wake of civil war; Tityrus, who speaks these final lines, has had his lands restored to him. Free to lounge and sing, he asks his heartbroken friend to be comforted by the plenitude of the moment — a landscape of unbroken pleasure.

This Night, at least, with me forget your Care;
Chestnuts and Curds and Cream shall be your fare:
The Carpet-ground shall be with Leaves o'respread;
And Boughs shall weave a Cov'ring for your Head.
For see yon sunny Hill the Shade extends;
And curling Smoke from Cottages ascends.

I've quoted Virgil in John Dryden's seventeenth-century translation — a translation that, for all of its obvious merits, was criticized by Wordsworth for its lack of "a tender heart" and "a lofty sense of moral dignity." In David Ferry's late twentieth-century translation of the eclogues, both these qualities are restored.

Nevertheless, tonight you might stay here
And rest yourself awhile on these green fronds;
The apples are ripe, the chestnuts are plump and mealy,
There's plenty of good pressed cheese you're welcome to.
Already there's smoke you can see from the neighbor's chimneys
And the shadows of the hill are lengthening as they fall.

Here, the landscape of pleasure is not unbroken; the shadows are longer, just as Virgil said they were. Tityrus asks Meliboeus to forget nothing. Instead, our knowledge of his loss colors at every moment our sense of the possibility of momentary pleasure. The pleasure of Ferry's translation is that, like Phillips's poems, it allows us to feel that experience and the loss of experience are almost impossible to distinguish. He allows us to feel the price of pleasure. This—not the stern opposition of song and suffering, of the personal and the civic—is the real tenderness of pastoral poetry.

For if pastoral poetry is about poetry, it registers most acutely poetry's limitations, not its power. "When I thought / Of singing of kings and battles," says Tityrus at the opening of the sixth eclogue, "the god Apollo / Tweaked my ear and said to me, 'A shepherd / Should feed fat sheep and sing a slender song.'" Is that slender song born of a retreat from social responsibility or of a recognition that singers are too often flattered by the exaggeration of their responsibility? Throughout the eclogues, there are moments when poetry seems imbued with Orphic power; in the eighth eclogue, during a singing contest between two shepherds, the cattle are "spellbound in the field, forgetting to graze." But in the ninth eclogue we are returned to a landscape of deprivation. Moeris meets Lycidas on the road to town and explains that (like Meliboeus in the first eclogue) his lands have been confiscated. Lycidas is shocked: "I was told Menalcas with his songs / Had saved the land." But Moeris's response is as tender as it is dignified: "Yes, that was the story; but what can music do / Against the weapons of soldiers?"

To read this admission of poetry's weakness as the "saddest moment" in the eclogue (the phrase is Patterson's) is to miss the tonal complexity that Ferry's translation of Virgil embodies so readily. For as the eclogue continues, Moeris and Lycidas continue to sing, or try to.

What was that song I heard you singing, alone,
The other night, under a cloudless sky?
I'd remember the tune . . . if I could remember the words . . .

"...Daphnis...tell me...why are you gazing only
At those old constellations in the sky?...
Look, Venus's grandson Caesar's star is rising...
The star that brings such joy to the ripening grain...
And deepens the colors of grapes on the sunny vines.
...Daphnis, plant your pear trees...years from now
The children of your children will gather the pears..."

This frayed, quavering song, half remembered, half forgotten, cannot restore Moeris's lands, but it can ease the long journey to town. Before they know it, the two shepherds are halfway there. "I'll carry the basket awhile," says Lycidas, "so you can sing." But even this attribution of a small amount of power to poetry is more than we can bear: "No more of that," responds Moeris, "let's just go on our way." Far from postulating a world immune to human suffering, a world in which poetry cures us, the eclogues never allow us to forget our losses.

This fragility is palpable in Ferry's translation not simply because the translator has been faithful to his text; it is clear because Ferry has remade the eclogues in a poetry that is itself as limpid and equivocal as the songs the shepherds sing. His blank verse is endlessly supple, and no two lines have quite the same rhythmic identity: "What was that song I heard you singing, alone, / The other night, under a cloudless sky?" The meaning of Ferry's Virgil is in the music: as a result, these exquisitely artificial poems speak intimately about the place of poetry in our time.

Carl Phillips's poems speak the same language. This is the first sentence of "The Gods Leaving."

That they carry away, with them,
vision—this isn't the worst of
the gods leaving: it's that they take

only half.

This is the second sentence.

There comes the hour
when — having lain long and favored
at the dark crossroads of Gift

and Desire; having as pliant
swans bested all arrows, no less
at ease with that wreckage than

with the glamour we have learned
to call pain given up to, until
wanted, a dream — we see it

was only, ever, our own bodies
by hands only our strong own
taken here, and here, down, ours

the mouths stalled at *Oh*, the eyes
clearing, enough to read or imagine
a reading for the shadows cast

to nobody's surprise by trees
theatrically there, shifting: *Don't
do this, don't do this* — always,

someone is too late.

Both the first and second sentences of "The Gods Leaving" are
typical of Phillips's hypotactic procedures, though the second is
more extreme: after the first independent clause ("There comes
the hour"), the second ("we see it") is delayed by eight lines of
subordination, making the sentence feel purposefully wayward,
a drama of delayed gratification made as much for the mouth as

the mind. Cleaved to the syntactical bone, the second sentence of "The Gods Leaving" would go something like this: *There comes an hour when we see it was only ever our own bodies.* The thought is not uninteresting (especially in a poem poised on the threshold of spiritual life), but the poem does not hold our attention necessarily because of what it says.

This is the third and final sentence.

> At
> that hour, because the gods aren't
> indifferent, we rise into what,
>
> already, is the new life — flat,
> general, "never for such as
> ourselves" — and it seems, at first,
>
> just the old one: rain, the fact
> of rain, so ordinary, stepping
> into it, I did not think to cry out.

These final lines provide the nominal subject matter of the poem, the event around which the utterance of the poem swirls: *I walked out into the rain one morning.* But "The Gods Leaving" does not only simply unfold the metaphorical implications of an ordinary moment of experience; it explains nothing, dispels no mystery. Instead, its highly interruptive syntax embodies the lush, inexplicable process by which each moment changes us forever.

Phillips is himself an accomplished classicist, and it is tempting to think of his sentences as the product of his intimate acquaintance with a highly inflected language. But it is even more revealing to note that while Phillips was teaching classical philology, his poems sounded very different. "When the Famous Black Poet speaks," begins a poem from his first book, *In the Blood*,

I understand

that his is the same unnervingly slow
rambling method of getting from A to B
that I hated in my father.

Reading *In the Blood*, it is clear (as Rachel Hadas puts it in her
introduction to the book) that Phillips "is a poet of color who is
erotically drawn to other men." Born in 1959, Phillips is the son
of a white mother, born in England, and an African-American
father, born in Alabama.

But while such information is simply assumed throughout
Pastoral, it is asserted in poems from *In the Blood* (although not,
as Phillips himself has admitted with chagrin, loudly enough to
please certain readers): the information functions not as part
of the texture of the utterance but as matter to be recounted.
Throughout *Pastoral*, the mind is so close to the world, the utterance so close to the event, that instead of offering a lucid presen-
tation of subject matter, the poems allow us to participate in the
drama of its discovery over time.

Does this mean that Phillips is hiding something? Stepping
away from his identity? As Virgil's *Eclogues* suggest, poets have
been on the defensive for several millennia, but the tendency to
judge a work of art in terms of the cultural relevance of its content has been exacerbated in the narrower world of American
poetry—a world that, despite all manner of stylistic comings and
goings, from Eliot to Lowell to Graham, still clings in the twenty-
first century to the notion that an authentic poem has nothing
to hide. "Am I a gay black man when roasting a chicken at home
for friends," asks Phillips in an essay called "A Politics of Mere
Being."

Sure. But that's not what I'm most conscious of, at the time.
Am I necessarily, then, stripped of political resonance at that
moment? Or is not the sharing of food with others a small so-

cial contract analogous to the contract of giving and taking—
of interaction—that we call citizenship in a democratic so-
ciety?

A poem would also be an example of such interaction, but like
Oppen, who wondered if there are situations in the life of a citizen that cannot honorably be met by poetry, Phillips is quietly
reluctant to assume that his poems exist inevitably in order to
register only the most potent markers of his identity.

Which is not to say that either Phillips or Oppen is merely
content with the limitations of poetry. Objections to what may
seem like the small world of the lyric poem rankle not because
they ought not to be raised; they feel high-handed because
they're unaware of the ways in which, at least since the time of
Virgil, lyric poetry has not only contained its own critique but
refused the moral glamor of the upper hand. "No longer do our
songs give pleasure now," says Gallus in the final eclogue. "I, too,
dislike it," says Marianne Moore. "Art just isn't worth that much,"
says Bishop. In poetry that's happening now, purpose can be indistinguishable from a disavowal of power.

XI

The Lyric Now

What kind of work do poems do? Why write them? These questions have been asked before, and no matter the answers, they'll be asked again. Throughout the twentieth century, many literary critics championed the notion of *close reading* as a way of defending poets and their admirers against charges of dilettantism: the act of reading a poem needed to be scrupulously empirical, quasi-scientific in the rigor of its attention. But to court the glamor of science is, in America, inevitably to play catch-up with the recent past, and the most defensive twenty-first-century literary critics have championed *distant reading* as a way of associating poetry with progress. Rather than reading the same poems over and over again, we need to crunch the data of millions of poems. "Between the pleasure and the knowledge of literature," says Franco Moretti, "there is no continuity." If only we'd stop reading them, poems might finally teach us something worth knowing.

Anyone might feel the allure of the new, the untried, the unexplored. Tourists take pains to distinguish their authentic experiences from the experiences of mere tourists, and this anxiety is as old as tourism itself: beginning as early as the eighteenth century, when the modern notion of tourism arose, the savvy tourist already defined himself as the traveler who took the road less traveled, even if no travelers had ever preceded him. What drives this fear of precedent? What happens if we're destined to see only the places anybody sees, to read again the poems anybody reads?

The knowledge we derive from our repeated experience of a

poem is ultimately the knowledge of our own mortality—the sense not only that we will be but also that we will have been. Anyone might want to evade this knowledge, but not everyone needs to go so far as to stop reading poems altogether in order to distinguish himself, and, in any case, unlike our knowledge of Milton, our knowledge of mortality cannot be evaded. But neither is it easily assumed. We exist fully in the present, suggests Heidegger in *Being and Time*, only by embracing the fate in store for everyone—not the new thing, but the oldest thing.

Poems enact that embrace repeatedly. What's the point of reading all 108 of Sir Philip Sidney's sonnets on the subject of his unrequited love for Penelope Rich?—or of reading all 131 of Tennyson's poems on the death of his friend Arthur Hallam? Why write poems about the dead at all? What do we learn from such poems that Orpheus didn't know? One of Moretti's distant reading projects catalogues the emotions associated with different locations in London throughout hundreds of English novels published between 1700 and 1900: the news is that the West End was associated with happiness while asylums and prisons were associated with fear. What news would a similarly distant reading of English elegies offer us?

Even Tennyson sometimes sounds exasperated throughout the 131 poems of *In Memoriam*. Three Christmas celebrations punctuate the temporal unfolding of the sequence, and in each of these poems Tennyson comes close to repeating himself verbatim: "And sadly fell our Christmas-eve"—"And calmly fell our Christmas-eve"—"And strangely falls our Christmas-eve." But if these lines might suggest that Tennyson craves the freedom implied by adverbial variation (*sadly, calmly, strangely*), the climactic poem of *In Memoriam* suggests that repetition without variation is his most hard-won achievement. It's a summer night; the poet and his friends are at peace.

While now we sang old songs that peal'd
   From knoll to knoll, where, couch'd at ease,

The white kine glimmer'd, and the trees
Laid their dark arms about the field.

But after his friends drift off to bed, the poet stays behind, re-reading the letters of his dead friend—letters he already knows well: "word by word, and line by line / The dead man touch'd me from the past." When the the trance passes, however, the poet is delivered not to deprivation but to the very condition of ordinary plenitude he experienced with his living friends.

The white kine glimmer'd, and the trees
Laid their dark arms about the field.

Far from offering an escape from "the steps of Time—the shocks of Chance— / The blows of Death," Tennyson's repeated experience of the letters returns him to a landscape of mortality, a landscape whose beauty can only be evoked by language that is itself repeated word by word.

"He who does not grasp that life is a repetition and that this is the beauty of life," says Søren Kierkegaard in *Repetition*, "has pronounced his own verdict and deserves nothing better than what will happen to him anyway—he will perish." What matters, as the long haul of *In Memoriam* not only describes but also embodies, is the struggle to maintain a productive awareness of mortality, which is anyway incontrovertible. "He alone is truly happy," says Kierkegaard, "who is not deluded into thinking that the repetition should be something new."

Such happiness could not easily be won; neither is it long lasting. But more discomfiting than the challenge of sheer repetition is an unalloyed contempt for its inevitability, which Tennyson also dramatizes. Facing the end of his long, adventurous life, the poignantly deluded speaker of "Ulysses" insists that it is "not too late to seek a newer world"—to "strive, to seek, to find, and not to yield." He is not happy, and he will yield. The wish that something truly unprecedented lies ahead of us is, in this attenuated form, the wish that we might never die.

If only by enticing us to read them repeatedly, poems exist to disabuse us of that wish; to read the climactic lines of *In Memoriam* is already to have read them twice. And yet the very fact that *In Memoriam* requires over one hundred poems to reach this acceptance of mortality suggests that, like anybody, poets need continually to be disabused of their wishes. As I mentioned in the preface, the modern American poets I've described in this book (Moore, Pound, Eliot, Williams, Stein) were variously invested in the effort to "make it new," as Pound said famously; but Pound himself emphasized that the most important word in that imperative, originally carved on a Chinese emperor's bathtub as a reminder about the power of daily hygiene, was "it": not the maker, not the novelty, but the thing that already exists. And as Michael North has shown in his history of the idea of novelty, Pound translated the phrase from a French translation of the original Confucian text—*fais-le de nouveau*, which might as easily be rendered into English as *do it again*. Is repeating something, doing it again, the same thing as rejuvenating something, making it new? "Why do we spend our lives like this," asks Sally Keith in *River House*, "naming / And re-naming the simplest human experience?"

River House, published in 2015, is a sequence of sixty-three sixteen-line poems on the death of the poet's mother, an event that seems shockingly unprecedented but, at the same time, unimaginable except as an event that has happened before and will happen again—not only to other people but to the poet herself, day after day, poem after poem. To live in these poems is to repeat oneself, there being nothing else to do: to wake up, watch the news, celebrate a birthday. And just as plainly, to live is to find oneself eating the pesto and prosciutto salad one's mother loved—to take one's mother's clothes to the recycling center where, only recently, she'd taken her own mother's clothes.

"Literature / Does nothing in the face of death," says Keith in the forty-seventh poem, repeating what she'd said forty poems earlier; neither does a pesto salad.

Clearly the author of these poems is not deluded into thinking that repetition should lead to something new. From the opening lines of *River House*, Keith has already assumed the posture Heidegger calls "being-toward-death"; the work of *River House* is not, however, to inhabit the posture (as it is in *In Memoriam*) but to sustain it by interrogating it. Literally, the poems are all over the place—Spain, Wyoming, Santa Fe, the south of France, as well as the house on the Rappahannock River, the house that is in every way a metonymic extension of the mother's being. More viscerally, this traveling takes place not only between poems but also within them: the lines leap wildly between disparate points in space and time, different registers of diction and tone, so the relentless return to the river house feels increasingly pleasurable, even as it is attended by the re-acknowledgment of loss.

Quotation, with which the poems are riven, is repetition. Memory is repetition, and so is the act of forgetting. Writing is repetition. Syntax is repetition: "She was dying and there was nothing we could do to stop it. / She was dying and before she was dead she had already left." By repeating itself repeatedly, the section Keith calls *"poem I wrote for my mother to say to me"* generates its very being on the page.

Sweet child I made of fire, sweet child, little fire
Bedeck the world with angels and ladders

Little mirror, I give you my last ounce of breath
I give you my breath to be emptied of life

Here, little fire, here, here
Little fire, lift my hand to feel a body emptied of life
Lift my hand, little mirror

Little fire, sweet child,
Put flowers on top of the table
Little fire, light candles in churches and cathedrals

Fire catches, sweet child
Bedeck the world with angels and ladders
Climb, little fire, climb higher and higher

I made you like this, little mirror, listen
As the wind shifts, listen to the smallest drops of water

Describers of the lyric poem from Horace (writing in the first
century BCE) to Jonathan Culler (writing two thousand years
later) have noted the lyric's strategies for staging its own immediacy, as if the poem were written in the time it takes to be read;
Keith relies repeatedly on the simple present (*I give you, I give
you*) and, even more potently, on the imperative (*lift my hand, lift
my hand*). But if, because of this rhetorical intensity, these lines
feel like the climactic section of *River House*, in fact the lines appear early in the sequence, far from its conclusion. The challenge
of *River House* is not to achieve this poem, not even to sustain
it, but to live with it, repeat it, put it in the past. The only words
available for use are words we've used before.

     What kind of work do poems do? Why write them? Every
poem poses these questions, but even more fabulously, every
poem answers them. Great poems answer them with an elo-
quence that can feel conclusive, once and for all. "Man is in love,
and loves what vanishes," wrote Yeats: "What more is there to
say?" Our need to keep writing or reading the next poem would
seem more explicable if we expected that new knowledge, new
answers, were forthcoming — if we imagined that every previous
answer, from Virgil to Yeats to Keith, had been insufficient. We
don't generally turn to Virgil because we've found Shakespeare
wanting, and I'm not aware of any poet ever writing a lasting
poem driven by contempt for a previous poem. We turn from

achievement to achievement, whether we're moving forward or backward in time.

Poems we love may disappoint us over time; anybody knows how it feels to return with trepidation to a particular poem or place. But when this happens, the fault lies not with the poem but with the rest of the world, which continues to hold out the facile promise of what Tennyson's death-defying Ulysses calls not just a "new" but a "newer" world—the more deserted beach, the more fulfilling love. It must be somewhere, and it is; it's right behind us, waiting to be experienced now.

Acknowledgments

Early versions of parts of these chapters appeared in the *Boston Review*, the *Nation*, *Salmagundi*, the *Southwest Review*, and the *Yale Review*. I'm grateful to the editors of these magazines for both their provocations and their support, and I'm especially grateful to John Palattella, who in his decade as literary editor of the *Nation* pushed my thinking in directions I would never have anticipated; I want also to remember Sandy McClatchy, who for many years welcomed me at the *Yale Review* with the elegance and generosity that distinguished him. Randolph Petilos guided the book through the University of Chicago Press, where I was honored to have my work read by Langdon Hammer and Katie Peterson, writers whose thinking I'd emulate eagerly. Matthew Bevis, Michael Collier, Kenneth Gross, and Donald Revell were a constant source of inspiration and advice, on the page and on the phone. For forty years, I've read Joanna Scott's pages as she's read mine: everything proceeds from this.

Bibliography

Adorno, Theodor. *Philosophy of Modern Music*. Translated by Anne Mitchell and Wesley Blomster. New York: Continuum, 2003.

————. *Prisms*. Translated by Samuel Weber and Shierry Weber. Cambridge, MA: MIT Press, 1981.

Alsadir, Nuar. *Fourth Person Singular*. Liverpool: Liverpool University Press, 2017.

Ashbery, John. *Collected Poems, 1956–1987*. Edited by Mark Ford. New York: Library of America, 2008.

————. *Selected Prose*. Edited by Eugene Richie. Ann Arbor: University of Michigan Press, 2004.

Baudelaire, Charles. *Les Fleurs du Mal: The Complete Text of The Flowers of Evil*. Translated by Richard Howard. Boston: D. R. Godine, 1982.

Bidart, Frank. *Half-Light: Collected Poems, 1965–2016*. New York: Farrar, Straus and Giroux, 2017.

————. *In the Western Night: Collected Poems, 1965–1990*. New York: Farrar, Straus and Giroux, 1990.

Bishop, Elizabeth. *Poems, Prose, and Letters, 1911–1979*. Edited by Robert Giroux and Lloyd Schwartz. New York: Library of America, 2008.

Burke, Kenneth. *Counter-Statement*. Berkeley: University of California Press, 1968.

Coleridge, Samuel Taylor. "On the Principles of Genial Criticism concerning the Fine Arts." In *Criticism: The Major Texts*, edited by Walter Jackson Bate, pp. 364–75. New York: Harcourt, 1970.

Culler, Jonathan. *Theory of the Lyric*. Cambridge, MA: Harvard University Press, 2015.

Dickinson, Emily. *The Poems of Emily Dickinson*. Edited by R. W. Franklin. 3 volumes. Cambridge, MA: Harvard University Press, 1998.

Donne, John. *Collected Poetry*. Edited by Ilona Bell. New York: Penguin, 2012.

Dryden, John. *The Works of John Dryden*. Edited by Edward Niles Hooker and H. T. Swedenberg Jr. Berkeley: University of California Press, 1956.

Eliot, T. S. *Complete Poems and Plays, 1909–1950*. New York: Harcourt, 1971.

———. "Eeldrop and Appleplex." *Little Review* 4 (May 1917): 7–11.

———. "Introduction." In Charlotte Eliot, *Savonarola*, pp. vii–xii. London: Cobden-Sanderson, 1926.

———. "Introduction." In Marianne Moore, *Selected Poems*, pp. vii–xiv. New York: Macmillan, 1935.

———. *The Letters of T. S. Eliot*. Edited by Valerie Eliot and Hugh Haughton. Volumes 1 and 2. New Haven: Yale University Press, 2011.

———. "A Sceptical Patrician." *Athenaeum* 4647 (1919): 361–62.

———. *Selected Essays, 1917–1932*. New York: Harcourt, 1960.

Emerson, Ralph Waldo. *Essays and Lectures*. Edited by Joel Porte. New York: Library of America, 1983.

Ferry, David, translator. *The Eclogues of Virgil*. New York: Farrar, Straus and Giroux, 1999.

Flaubert, Gustave. *The Letters of Gustave Flaubert, 1830–1857*. Translated and edited by Francis Steegmuller. Cambridge, MA: Harvard University Press, 1981.

Gordon, Lyndall. *T. S. Eliot: An Imperfect Life*. New York: Norton, 1999.

Graham, Jorie. *Never: Poems*. New York: Ecco, 2002.

———. *Swarm*. New York: Ecco, 2000.

Hardy, Thomas. Notebook entry, 17 October 1896. In *The Life and Work of Thomas Hardy*, edited by Michael Milgate. London: Macmillan, 1984.

Heidegger, Martin. *Being and Time*. Translated by John Macquarrie and Edward Robinson. New York: Harper, 1962.

Hoffman, Eric. "A Poetry of Action: George Oppen and Communism." *American Communist History* 6 (2007): 1–28.

Jarrell, Randall. *Poetry and the Age*. New York: Vintage, 1953.

Johnson, Clifton. *What to See in America*. New York: Macmillan, 1919.

Keats, John. *The Letters of John Keats, 1814–1821*. Edited by H. E. Rollins. 2 volumes. Cambridge, MA: Harvard University Press, 1958.

Keith, Sally. *River House*. Minneapolis: Milkweed, 2015.

Kierkegaard, Søren. *Fear and Trembling; Repetition*. Edited and translated by Howard Hong and Edna Hong. Princeton, NJ: Princeton University Press, 1983.

Leavell, Linda. *Holding On Upside Down: The Life and Work of Marianne Moore*. New York: Farrar, Straus and Giroux, 2013.

Lowell, Robert. *Collected Poems*. Edited by Frank Bidart and David Gewanter with DeSales Harrison. New York: Farrar, Straus and Giroux, 2003.

———. "The Mills of the Kavanaughs." *Kenyon Review* 12 (1959): 1–39.

Moody, A. D. *Ezra Pound: Poet*. Volume 1, *The Young Genius, 1885–1920*. New York: Oxford University Press, 2007.

Moore, Marianne. *New Collected Poems*. Edited by Heather Cass White. New York: Farrar, Straus and Giroux, 2017.

———. *The Selected Letters of Marianne Moore*. Edited by Bonnie Costello. New York: Knopf, 1997.

———. *Selected Poems*. Edited by T. S. Eliot. New York: Macmillan, 1935.

Moretti, Franco. *Distant Reading*. New York: Verso, 2013.

North, Michael. *Novelty: A History of the New*. Chicago: University of Chicago Press, 2013.

Oppen, George. *New Collected Poems*. Edited by Michael Davidson. New York: New Directions, 2002.

———. *The Selected Letters of George Oppen*. Edited by Rachel Blau DuPlessis. Durham, NC: Duke University Press, 1990.

———. *Selected Prose, Daybooks, and Papers*. Edited by Stephen Cope. Berkeley: University of California Press, 2007.

Patterson, Annabel. *Pastoral and Ideology*. Berkeley: University of California Press, 1987.

Phillips, Carl. *In the Blood*. Boston: Northeastern University Press, 1992.

————. *Pastoral*. Saint Paul: Graywolf, 2000.

————. "A Politics of Mere Being." *Poetry* 209 (December 2016): 295–310.

Pound, Ezra. *The Cantos*. New York: New Directions, 1975.

————. *Literary Essays of Ezra Pound*. Edited by T. S. Eliot. New York: New Directions, 1968.

————. *Personae: The Shorter Poems of Ezra Pound*. Edited by Lea Baechler and A. Walton Litz. New York: New Directions, 1990.

————. *The Selected Letters of Ezra Pound, 1907–1941*. Edited by D. D. Paige. New York: New Directions, 1971.

Rankine, Claudia. *Citizen: An American Lyric*. Minneapolis: Graywolf, 2014.

Smith, Patti. *Babel*. New York: Putnam, 1978.

————. *Just Kids*. New York: Ecco, 2010.

————. *M Train*. New York: Knopf, 2015.

————. *Woolgathering*. New York: New Directions, 1992.

Snell, Bruno. *The Discovery of the Mind*. Translated by T. G. Rosenmeyer. New York: Dover, 1982.

Stein, Gertrude. *Writings, 1903–1932*. Edited by Catharine Stimpson and Harriet Chessman. New York: Library of America, 1998.

Tennyson, Alfred. *The Poems of Tennyson*. Edited by Christopher Ricks. London: Longmans, 1969.

Thomson, Virgil. *Music Chronicles, 1940–1954*. Edited by Tim Page. New York: Library of America, 2014.

————. *The State of Music and Other Writings*. Edited by Tim Page. New York: Library of America, 2016.

Wordsworth, William. "Letter of 7 November 1805." In *Dryden: The Critical Heritage*, edited by James and Helen Kinsley, pp. 323–25. New York: Barnes and Noble, 1971.

Williams, William Carlos. *The Collected Poems of William Carlos Williams*. Edited by A. Walton Litz and Christopher MacGowan. 2 volumes. New York: New Directions, 1988.

Winnicott, D. W. *Playing and Reality*. New York: Routledge, 1971.

Yeats, W. B. *The Poems*. Volume 1 of *The Collected Works of W. B. Yeats*. Edited by Richard Finneran. New York: Macmillan, 1989.

Index